EAST

LONDON

CHARLES

SAUMAREZ

SMITH

WAPPING SHADW

LIMEHOUSE ISLE

ALDGATE WHITEC

MILE END BOW E

STRATFORD

SHOREDITCH E

HOXTON HAGGE

VELL RATCLIFFE

OF DOGS POPLAR

HAPEL STEPNEY

ROMLEY-BY-BOW

PITALFIELDS

ETHNAL GREEN

STON HACKNEY

Introduction / 7

Wapping /11
Shadwell /37
Ratcliffe /47
Limehouse /63
Isle of Dogs /89
Poplar /105
Aldgate /119
Whitechapel /125
Stepney /143
Mile End /195
Bow /207
Bromley-by-Bow /215
Stratford /221
Spitalfields /237
Shoreditch /275
Bethnal Green /285
Hoxton /309
Haggerston /315
Hackney /327

Further Reading / 350
Acknowledgments / 351

The East End, which can become on close acquaintance almost the most exciting of London atmospheres, is the most difficult for tourists, particularly foreign tourists, to 'work' alone. A personal guide is the real answer, preferably someone who has lived in the East End and knows it backwards.

David Piper, *The Companion Guide to London*, 1968

I began to explore East London in 1971, when I was teaching English and mathematics at Westminster Abbey Choir School. My brother had lent me his copy of *Nairn's London*, with a picture on the cover of Ian Nairn standing on the deck of a double-decker bus, and I would spend the afternoons off and weekends exploring on my own, all those pubs and cemeteries. It was then that I first visited the great Hawksmoor churches that preside so majestically over Spitalfields, Shadwell and Limehouse, and it was then that I first saw Wickham's Department Store in the Mile End Road, because of Nairn's enthusiasm for the way that Spiegelhalter's had refused to sell up, retaining their small shop in the middle of Wickham's much grander façade – 'a perennial triumph', as Nairn described it, 'for the little man, the bloke who won't conform'. I remember obtaining an early edition of *Time Out* with a list of the ten best walks in London and walking from Tottenham Hale down the River Lea and also from Greenwich Hospital along the Thames travelling east to the Blackwall Tunnel, a walk that Nairn recommends taking in the other direction. It was another country out beyond the Tower of London, of bleak urban wasteland and industrial dereliction waiting to be discovered.

I retained this interest as an undergraduate studying neo-classical architecture in Cambridge, when I visited Greek Revival churches in the East End, including Clapton and Wanstead, with Romilly, my then girlfriend, now wife.

In 1982, we were living in an attic flat in Trinity Church Square in Southwark. Romilly was working as a bookbinder in the basement. She needed a new studio. We decided to look in the East End. We took the tube to Aldgate, where we would sometimes go for a meal at Bloom's, the great Jewish restaurant next door to the Whitechapel Art Gallery where the service was so fast that one couldn't linger, and set off walking up the Mile End Road. Just past the Trinity almshouses, there was an old-fashioned estate agent, Prevost & Co., which specialized in commercial properties. In the window, it had the sales particulars of a terrace house in Newell Street – once known as Church Row – in front of the west tower of St Anne's, Limehouse.

We set off at once, rang the front door bell, and were greeted by Romilly's paper dealer, who was living in Number 13 while he restored the house next door.

Ever since, we have lived in the East End, shopping in the Tesco down a road by the Three Mills off the old motorway in Bow, and in Asda next to the Mudchute on the Isle of Dogs. Our children went to Stepney Greencoat Primary School off Salmon Lane, and we watched the towers of Canary Wharf rise out of the bathroom window. Each morning I would walk through the churchyard of St Anne's, Limehouse, to catch the Docklands Light Railway to go to work at the Victoria and Albert Museum. On Saturdays, I would go shopping in Rogg's, Cannon Street Road's long-gone Jewish delicatessen.

We lived in the East End, but I did not study it. It was only much later that, in walking along its canals and witnessing the rapid process of urban change, I developed an idea of trying to document and record the topography. In February 2014, I started writing a blog in which I would jot down my observations of things I saw or places I was visiting, many of them close to where we live on the Mile End Road in Stepney, which is, and always has been, at the heart of the historic East End. I described the bits and pieces that make up East London – shops, churches, backstreets, graveyards; the details which determine the character of each area – and recorded them by taking photographs on my mobile phone.

In preparing the blog entries for publication, I have abolished many of the casual and contingent references to the weather, and have ordered them more systematically, according to the old East End parishes, arranging them logically as far as possible: beginning at the Tower and moving eastwards along the river, then from Aldgate eastwards to Stratford, and finally from Spitalfields north and east to Hackney. I have not covered much to the east of the River Lea, since I explored most of the territory by walking. I have added short introductions to each of the neighbourhoods in order to give a broader historical context to the more detailed entries. But at its heart the book remains, as it set out to be, a series of *ad hoc* observations and reflections on individual buildings and how they reveal the process of historical change.

This book is not a lament. I respect the process of change – the gradual, and in some places rapid, gentrification, the ways in which Spitalfields has been transformed from an area of downbeaten Georgian houses into an epicentre of fashion. Gentrification is creeping into Stepney like a slow tide coming down the Mile End Road. Canary Wharf is now an established financial district. Limehouse Basin, once a large and empty piece of open water where we enjoyed open-air performance art, is now a marina. It's hard to walk up the Regent's Canal at the weekend because of the hordes of cyclists. You can no longer take an early morning swim in Victoria Park, and there are no longer squats in Bishopsway. Bethnal Green Town Hall is a hotel owned by a Singaporean entrepreneur.

East London is now not an area of dereliction, but of rapidly rising house prices, as old warehouses are torn down and new housing blocks rise up. It's changing fast, and this book is as much as anything a way of recording and documenting this process of change. It will, I hope, encourage people to look around them and enjoy, as I have, the complexities of history, architecture and neighbourhood that constitute the visual experience of the East End.

WAPPING

Wapping Alleyways /14 /A
Phoenix Wharf /20 /B
Wapping Pier Head /22 /C
St John, Wapping /22 /D
St Peter's, Wapping Lane /24 /E
Wapping Pumping Station /24 /F
Wapping Market /26
St George-in-the-East /28 /G
Nature Study Museum /30 /G
Wilton's Music Hall /32 /H
John Fisher Street /34 /J

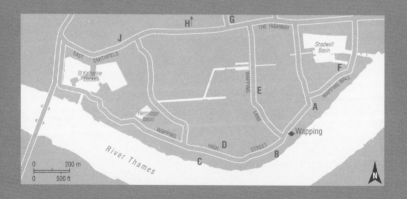

First among the riverside neighbourhoods, and the first
to be gentrified, is **Wapping**, tucked into a gentle bend of
the Thames as it snakes eastwards – close to the Tower,
but in an odd way unrelated to it because of the absence of
roads connecting it to the City. This has always meant that
Wapping's character has been determined more by the river
than by its proximity to the City. It was traditionally an area
of boats arriving and docking in the Port of London, home to
the rough trades associated with the temporary lodging of
seamen, the opportunities for sailors to lose their earnings
in the pubs that lined the High Street – including the Town
of Ramsgate and Prospect of Whitby, both of which survive.
In the 1970s, when the docks closed down, it was colonized
by artists who held parties in the wharves and, in the 1980s,
the wharves began to be turned into luxury flats. But it still
retains a curious sense of isolation, with areas of greenery
around the parish church of St John and Hussey's, a good
old-fashioned butcher, in Wapping Lane.

Wapping Alleyways

One can get down to the
Thames by way of two small
alleyways off Wapping High
Street. The first is alongside
New Crane Wharf.

Wapping

Wapping Alleyways

The second is next to the
Town of Ramsgate pub,
where, again, one can get
down to the river and look
across to Rotherhithe and
upriver to the Shard.

Wapping

Phoenix Wharf

Phoenix Wharf, one of the best preserved of the riverside warehouses, is less poshed up and neo-Victorianized than the others. It was designed by Sydney Smirke RA, the architect of the Royal Academy's exhibition galleries, in 1840.

There is a nice Victorian
tenement block just north
of Wapping High Street
on Brewhouse Lane.

Wapping Pier Head

I've always admired Wapping
Pier Head, the original
entrance to London Dock,
with its Regency houses.

St John, Wapping

The tower of St John,
Wapping, was designed
by Joel Johnson in 1756,
and next door St John's
Old School was erected
by subscription in 1760.

Wapping

St Peter's,
Wapping Lane

Further north is the Anglo-
Catholic stronghold of
St Peter's, Wapping Lane,
as high now as when it
was built.

Wapping Pumping
Station

I can't help but lament the
closure of Wapping Pumping
Station, which was opened
in 1977 as an arts venue with
attached restaurant, called
The Wapping Project. It was
an early sign of East End
revival, on a lease with a
restrictive covenant granted
by the London Docklands
Development Corporation.
It has now been closed and
apparently sold to a property
developer. As Rowan Moore
pointed out in the *Observer*,
it represents a considerable
impoverishment of the
public realm.

The Pumping Station, built in
1890 by the London Hydraulic
Power Co., has lost none of
its old industrial glory.

Wapping

Wapping Market

I was just remarking
how difficult it was to buy
good-quality bacon (the
decline of the butcher/the
feebleness of supermarket
bacon), when, lo and behold,
a farmers' market rose up
on the wharves of London
Dock. It was a new farmers'
market, sadly short-lived, just
next to Wapping Pumping
Station: fresh fish available
in boxes, organic vegetables,
flat bread, van food and Ruby
Violet's handmade ice cream.

Wapping

St George-in-the-East

St George-in-the-East
is the Hawksmoor church
I know least well, set back
as it is above The Highway:
more mannered and complex
than St Anne's, Limehouse,
less monumental than Christ
Church, Spitalfields.

This is the tower from the south.

The west tower, with its
octagonal finials.

A view of the church from
the east showing the circular
Roman apse.

Nature Study
Museum

The Nature Study Museum is
in the grounds of St George-
in-the-East. It's an odd little
building, nearly completely
derelict, originally built as a
mortuary chapel where coffins
were put before their transfer
to a public cemetery. In 1904,
it was converted into the Nature
Study Museum by an eager
young curator, Miss Kate
Hall, to introduce the local
poor to the world of nature,
housing tanks of frogs, toads,
newts and salamanders,
and beehives outside. When
she died, the building was
described as a 'fairy house
in an oasis', but the resident
monkey took to biting children
and the museum was closed
during the Second World War.

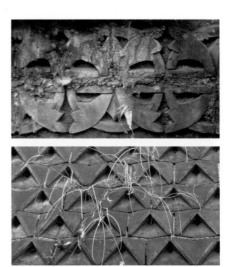

Wapping

Wilton's Music Hall

The first time we went
back to Wilton's Music
Hall since its renovation
by Tim Ronalds, funded
by the Heritage Lottery
Fund, we were worried,
because nothing is harder
to restore than crumbling
magnificence (see what
happened to Christ Church,
Spitalfields). But, miracle of
miracles, it is the same, only
better: just as run down and
shabby, with a bar next door
to the theatre and a mass
of old wood and peeling
paint, but now with a lift
(we were its first users).
We saw a performance
of *l'Ospedale*, a hitherto
unknown mid-seventeenth-
century opera by an obscure
composer on the problems
of seventeenth-century
medicine, updated as a
commentary on the NHS:
a production by a young
and newly formed musical
collective called Solomon's
Knot.

Wapping

John Fisher Street

Níall McLaughlin has put up
a new building in among some
classic Peabody buildings
just short of the Tower of
London on John Fisher Street
(previously Glasshouse
Street). The original estate
consists of nine buildings,
each labelled according to a
letter of the alphabet, designed
by H.A. Darbishire and built
in 1880. Níall McLaughlin has
added a thin, free-standing
block, in appropriately austere
pale brick, not aping the
surroundings, but in
sympathy with them.

Wapping

SHADWELL

St Paul's, Shadwell /40 /A
Shadwell Basin /42 /B
Cable Street /44 /C

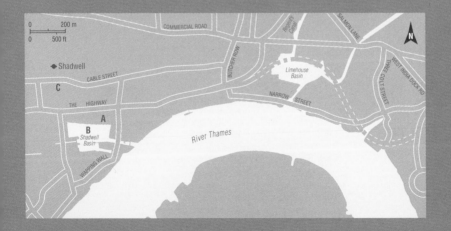

As the Thames curves round towards the Isle of Dogs, the first of the neighbourhoods is **Shadwell**, which now scarcely survives – obliterated by the creation of the King Edward VII Park – other than as a station on the Docklands Light Railway. It was a creation of the seventeenth century, when land values were high and access to the river valuable, and by the end of the eighteenth century it had a distillery, three coal wharves and two docks. In 1800, J.P. Malcolm, the topographer, described the neighbourhood as having 'thousands of useful tradesmen, artisans and mechanicks, and numerous watermen … but their homes and workshops will not bear description; nor are the streets, courts, lanes, and alleys, by any means inviting'. Nowadays, I'm not sure that anyone aspires to live in Shadwell. The park never quite works as an urban space, being too municipalized, although it's better now that it has an organic aspect to it. Cable Street, where the station is, is long and mostly unglamorous, apart from the row of houses north of the church. And the area is cut through by the roar of traffic heading east along The Highway, which was a Roman road.

St Paul's, Shadwell

St Paul's, Shadwell, lurks
beyond the high wall of the
old London Dock across
Shadwell Basin. One of the
first of the Commissioners'
churches, it was designed
by John Walters, who
died in 1821, the year after
the church opened, aged
39. It replaced what was
known as the Church of
Sea Captains and was
described in Walters'
obituary in the *Gentleman's
Magazine* as 'simply neat,
and elegantly chaste'.

Just west of the church are
surviving dock cottages,
a reminder of what Shadwell
once was.

Shadwell

Shadwell Basin

I thought Ted Cullinan
had designed Shadwell
Basin. I've discovered that
it was designed by Richard
MacCormac or one of his
partners in an early, and
good, example of docklands
rebuilding from the first
days of regeneration (it
was completed in 1987),
a miscellaneous example
of classical elements, with
Venetian arches and split
pediments, half replicating
early nineteenth-century
industrial buildings.

Shadwell

Cable Street

Cable Street was the heartland of the old East End: bombed in the war, the Tarling Estate erected after it, but still with good early nineteenth-century houses in a row just north of the church.

The old Town Hall, designed by G.A. Wilson in 1860.

The Tarling estate.

These are some of
the original houses.

RATCLIFFE

Albert Gardens /52 /A
Arbour Square /54 /B
Royal Foundation of St Katharine /56 /C
Half Moon Theatre /60 /D

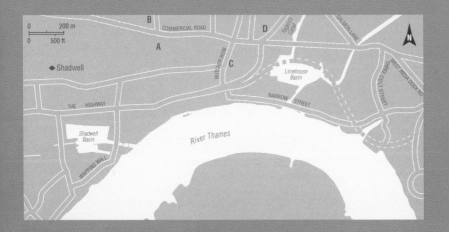

Beyond Shadwell, and closely related to it, is **Ratcliffe**, centred
on the Ratcliffe Highway (now known simply as The Highway),
which runs along a sandstone ridge and was historically the
main route along the river. It was intersected by Butcher Row,
which connected Stepney to the river. Ratcliffe was the first
of the communities north of the river to develop ship-building
and its related industries, such as the manufacture of ropes
and anchors, and included a shipyard owned in the early
seventeenth century by Phineas Pett. By the nineteenth
century, the riverside teemed with wharves, warehouses and
ship-builders' yards, of which only a fragment of Free Trade
Wharf now survives, and was densely populated by mariners,
wharfingers and dockers.

Ratcliffe

There is a sign set into the wall on Salmon Lane (once Sermon Lane) by the junction with Barnes Street that demarcates the parish boundary.

White Horse Road.

This is some of the nearby
housing in Aston Street.

Over the years, Ratcliffe's
final 'e' has come and gone.

Albert Gardens

Just off Commercial Road,
halfway to Limehouse, is
Albert Gardens. A square
of nearly perfect, neat,
early Victorian houses,
it was laid out in the 1840s
with a garden in the middle
by the Metropolitan Public
Gardens Association.
A sculpture of a 'Shepherd
Boy' with sheaf and sickle,
dated 1903 and bought
in Paris, stands in the centre
of the square.

Ratcliffe

Arbour Square

Arbour Square is just north
of Commercial Road, laid
out in 1819 and built as a
consequence of Commercial
Road being driven through
the neighbourhood to give
direct access to the docks.
Two sides of the square
retain terrace houses.

The third side was knocked
down early in the twentieth
century to create Raine's
Foundation School, designed
in full Wrenaissance style by
Herbert Ellis.

Royal Foundation
of St Katharine

Ever since we first moved to Limehouse in the early 1980s I have been intrigued by the Royal Foundation of St Katharine, which occupies a large site on Butcher Row, but always seems impenetrable.

I discovered that its entrance is at the back, so I asked to see the chapel. It's an ancient foundation, originally established by Queen Matilda in 1147 by the Tower of London. The creation of St Katharine Docks displaced the foundation to Regent's Park, and after the war they moved to the site of the old parish church of St James, Ratcliffe, which was bombed in 1940, taking over the eighteenth-century vicarage. The chapel and surrounding retreat were designed by R.E. Enthoven in good Festival of Britain style.

The Master's House was built
in 1795 for Matthew Whiting,
a sugar refiner and Director
of the Phoenix Assurance
Company, which oversaw
the reconstruction of the
neighbourhood after a fire
in 1794.

The chapel.

Ratcliffe

One of the surviving
monuments from the church.

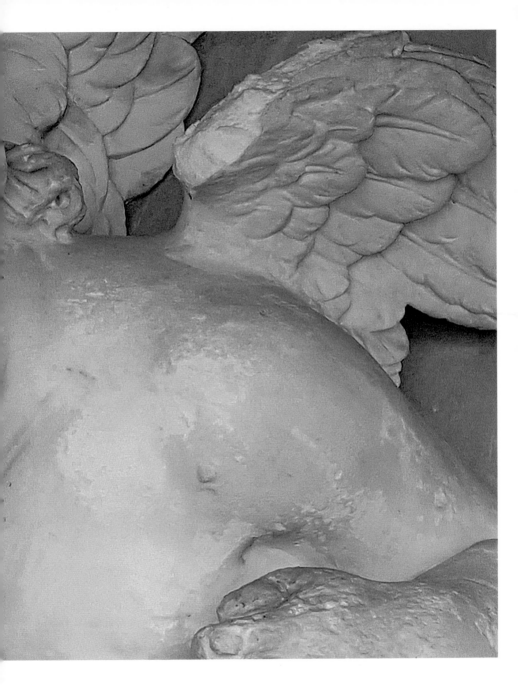

Ratcliffe

Half Moon Theatre

I was walking across York
Square when I spotted in the
distance the rooftop lettering
of the Half Moon Theatre
shining in the morning sun.

I had never noticed it
before. It's what survives
of the original Half Moon
Theatre, which used to be
in premises just beyond
Stepney Green tube station,
but was closed in 1990 and
turned into a Wetherspoon
pub. The building that this
young people's theatre
now occupies in White
Horse Road was originally
the local District Board of
Works, designed in 1862 by
C.R. Dunch.

Ratcliffe

LIMEHOUSE

York Square /66 /A
Commercial Road /68
Roy Square /70 /B
Barleymow Estate /70 /C
Three Colt Street /72 /D
West India Dock /72 /E
Limehouse Basin /74
The Mission /76 /G
Limehouse Town Hall /78 /H
St Anne's, Limehouse /80 /J
Regent's Canal /82 /K
The Futuro House /86 /L

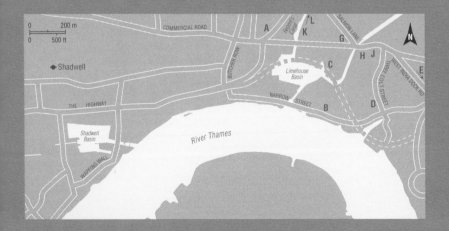

In the crook of the river as it turns sharply southwards towards Greenwich is **Limehouse**, a proud parish originally independent of London, specializing in ship-building and limeburning for the building industry, which gave the village its name. By the seventeenth century, there was a small shipyard, where Pepys observed the building of 'herring busses' – boats used for herring fishing – as well as the ropewalks to the north of Fore Street, which gave the name to Ropemaker's Fields. In the early eighteenth century, the great church of St Anne's, Limehouse, was built as a way of bringing Christianity to an area ill-served by churches and regarded by parliament as heathen. The Limehouse Cut was created in the early 1770s to connect the Thames to the River Lea, and a row of houses was built to the west of the churchyard. By the nineteenth century the area was heavily industrial, with a settled Chinese community who were later to run laundries and restaurants. In the 1950s, fashionable folk from the West End lived on Narrow Street by the river, including, briefly, Lucian Freud and Jacob Rothschild. David Owen bought a house on the river in 1965 and in 1981 it was the site of the Limehouse Declaration, establishing the Social Democratic Party. Meanwhile, David Lean had moved into a large warehouse site on Narrow Street and Tom Brent had built a small row of postmodern houses in the grounds of the Prince of Wales Sea Training Hostel for Boys, which was run as a quasi-commune by Nick Wates in the 1970s. In the 1980s, big new developments were built round the Limehouse Basin, some badly designed, but some, like the row of houses on Narrow Street opposite The Grapes by Proctor & Matthews, extremely well considered. Limehouse is now yuppified, the new developments absorbed, Ropemaker's Fields providing a mature park, and one can walk along the river to Canary Wharf.

York Square

York Square, a neat East End
Square built by the Mercers'
Company in the mid-1820s
and taken over by the GLC
in 1973, is all of a piece apart
from a certain amount of
rebuilding after the war.
There was a recent campaign
to save the Queen's Head as
a community resource and
not sell it, as so many of the
other local pubs have been.
And they're now doing up
Flamborough Walk, one of
those secret, gated snickets
that are such a feature of the
East End.

Flamborough Walk.

York Square.

The Queen's Head.

Limehouse

Commercial Road

They've let the shops in the Commercial Road run down. It used to be where the local gun shop was, and Callegari's Restaurant, once a roadside café, is now derelict. One could buy fish from a fishmongers that was open to all the exhaust fumes from the main road, and bread round the corner at Wall's. But now the whole block is vacant, awaiting redevelopment.

I always liked the lettering on The Emporium.

Round the corner, one could buy fruit and veg.

This was Callegari's.

Roy Square

Roy Square (originally named after its developer and now called 'The Watergarden' after the long pond inside it) is an early example of docklands housing, designed by Ian Ritchie and built in 1988. It wasn't helped by being used for the displacement of tenants from the Barleymow Estate five years later.

Barleymow Estate

The Barleymow Estate (called Barleymow because it occupies the site of the original 1730 Taylor Walker brewery) sits behind the false hill of Ropemaker's Fields.

Three Colt Street

I have long been intrigued by
the angel and blue columns
on the house at the corner
of Three Colt Street, which
were put there by the artist
Peter Fink. Designed by
the artist John Buckley,
famous for putting a shark
through the roof of his house
in Oxford, the angel was a
portrait of Peter's son Ezra,
aged three.

West India Dock

The original gateway to
West India Dock looks
as if it needs a haircut.

Limehouse Basin

Limehouse Basin is much shrunk from what it once was. It was originally constructed as the Regent's Canal Dock in 1812, but the Regent's Canal itself was not completed for another eight years, by which time the dock had been enlarged to accommodate the coasters that brought food and coal from East Anglia and the north of England to feed and heat the greedy capital. By the mid-nineteenth century, it was already too small for the new steamships and so was used instead for the construction of lifeboats. When we moved to Limehouse in the early 1980s, it was much larger than it is now, a disused expanse of vacant water, subsequently part filled in and converted into a marina.

Limehouse

The Mission

When we lived in Limehouse,
we inherited from John
Chesshyre, the previous
owner of our house, an
architectural drawing for the
Empire Memorial Sailor's
Hostel, or 'The Mission',
which was designed by
Thomas Brammall Daniel
and Horace W. Parnacott.
It opened in 1924 with beds
for 205 sailors in cabins.
It's a fine building, with a
grandiose stripped-down,
perpendicular frontispiece.
Rather amazingly, in 1960 the
building was the location for
the 4th Conference of the
Situationist International,
a group of revolutionary
Marxists led by Guy Debord,
who pioneered the study of
psychogeography.

T. BRAMMALL DANIEL. F.R.I.B.A.
AND
HORACE W. PARNACOTT. A.R.I.B.A.
ARCHITECTS. 1923.
G.E. WALLIS & SONS LTD. BVILDERS.

Limehouse

Limehouse Town Hall

I often pass Limehouse
Town Hall, a remnant of
nineteenth-century civic
pomp backing onto the
churchyard of St Anne's.
Built in 1879 to 'do honour
to the parish of Limehouse',
it was lavishly equipped
and licensed for dancing.
The site of a major speech
by then Chancellor of the
Exchequer, Lloyd George, in
defence of his 1909 'People's
Budget' and of Attlee's
election victories, the
building was occupied by the
National Museum of Labour
History in the 1980s before
that institution decamped
to Manchester. It's now used
for bicycle maintenance and
is on the Buildings at Risk
register.

Limehouse

St Anne's, Limehouse

I deeply love St Anne's, Limehouse, one of the greatest of Hawksmoor's East End churches. It's solid and serious, and like a church in Rome, a great baroque monument in an area that was once shipyards and slums. The bulk of the church is quite simple, with round-headed windows and a barn-like interior. Hawksmoor put all his effort into the sculptural west end.

Regent's Canal

The Regent's Canal is the
artery that connects the
Thames to the Midlands.
It looked particularly
beautiful with more barges
than usual when the stretch
north of Limehouse Basin
was being dredged.

People are often out in force
on the towpath – walkers,
runners, barge-owners.

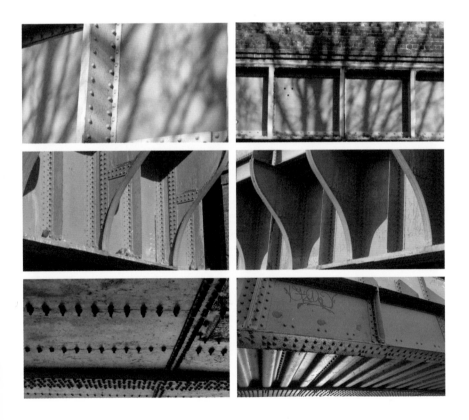

Each of the bridges across the
canal is numbered and named.

The Futuro House

The Futuro House looks
as if it has landed like an alien
spacecraft on the roof of
Matt's Gallery, next door to
the Ragged School Museum
on the Regent's Canal.
The first Futuro House was
designed in the 1960s in
Finland as a ski cabin, and
they were then manufactured
as cheap homes. But they
were so unpopular that they
were subjected to drive-by
shootings in the United
States. This one was found
ruined in South Africa and
has been meticulously
restored by architect Craig
Barnes, maybe as an example
of cheap manufactured
homes.

Limehouse

ISLE OF DOGS

Canary Wharf /92 /A
Crossrail Place /96 /B
Mudchute /98 /C
Compass Point /98 /D
Storm Water Pumping Station /100 /E
Greenwich Foot Tunnel /100 /F

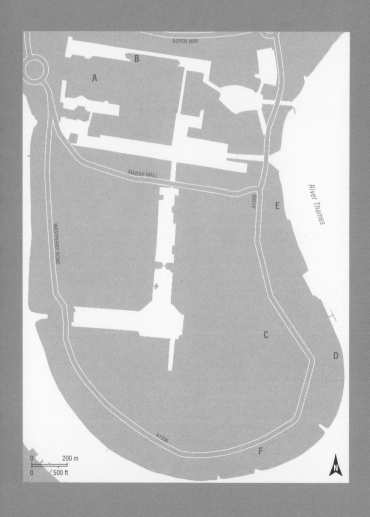

The **Isle of Dogs**, moated by a long southwards loop of the Thames, was once wild and independent hunting territory. Originally known as Stepney Marsh and with a few desolate windmills, it was cut off from the rest of the East End by the construction of the West India Docks across its neck at the beginning of the nineteenth century. In the early twentieth century, it was remote from the rest of London, but the Chapel House Estate was laid out after the First World War in order to provide Homes for Heroes. In the 1970s, Michael Barraclough, a surgeon at St Thomas's, moved from Narrow Street to the southern tip where he designed a house for himself immediately opposite the Royal Naval Hospital, Greenwich, and became a local community activist, responsible for preserving Mudchute Farm. There was fierce resistance to the arrival of the London Docklands Development Corporation in 1981 and there used to be large posters objecting to the arrival of big money. But big money moved in nevertheless. Michael von Clemm and G. Ware Travelstead, energetic entrepreneurs who were respectively chairman of and property advisor for Credit Suisse First Boston, saw the opportunity for a new city following the model of the developments on the Boston waterfront. The result was a grand new development in Canary Wharf, laid out as if it was a new Chicago, in pastiche American style. Not everyone admires it, but, as a neighbour of ours at the time said, it's better that it emulates Manhattan than Croydon.

Canary Wharf

One only has to blink and
another six sleek office
blocks have gone up. The
original Cesar Pelli tower
that used to be so dominant
in the urban landscape is
itself now dwarfed. Heron
Quays, the original low-rise
scheme of red-framed
offices and small business
units designed by Nick
Lacey, has gone. Even Piers
Gough's Cascades, the
original housing block on
the river, is overwhelmed.
The language of Chicagoan
classicism has been
replaced by glass and steel.

This is one's first view of
the Cesar Pelli tower from
the east.

Dundee Wharf looked
unnecessarily mannered
when it first went up, but
has worn well.

Foster for Citigroup.

Skidmore, Owings and   Kohn Pedersen Fox.
Merrill. Described by
Pevsner as clumsy.

And this is what it used to
be like.

Crossrail Place

A new Norman Foster
building has been attached
to the north side of Canary
Wharf and will in due course
house its Crossrail station.
It's a mixture of ballooning
high tech and craft detailing in
the engineered wooden struts:
currently a bit bland because
it's not yet functioning, but
with an elaborate antipodean
roof garden.

Isle of Dogs

Mudchute

I like the false rusticity of the Mudchute (actually, at least in its allotments, a remarkably effective illusion of rusticity).

Compass Point

Relatively early in the development of docklands, Jeremy Dixon created a miniature townscape of houses, including a crescent and Dutch gables.

Isle of Dogs

Storm Water Pumping Station

John Outram's magnificent
postmodern, but essentially
neo-romantic, pumping station.

Greenwich Foot Tunnel

I was told that the
Greenwich Foot Tunnel had
closed. This is completely
untrue. If anything, it's
been done up, with a new
automated lift. We used
to regard it as the means
of escape to middle-class
Greenwich where there
were teashops and the
Park. Construction began
in 1899 and was completed
in 1902. There's a grand list
of prohibitions, but no-one,
particularly cyclists, takes
much notice of them.

Isle of Dogs

Isle of Dogs

POPLAR

St Matthias Churchyard /108 /A
Robin Hood Gardens /112 /B
Balfron Tower /114 /C
St Mary and St Joseph /116 /D

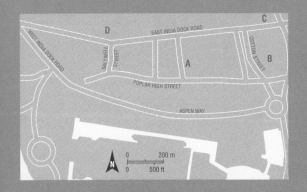

Poplar was a hamlet on the road from Limehouse to Blackwall, with its own small proprietary chapel, St Matthias, established by the East India Company to serve the workers in its dock and spare them having to walk across the fields to Stepney church. It was indeed dominated by the East India Company, whose ships would arrive laden with silks and teas, and whose dock was run in the seventeenth century by Henry Johnson, a boat-builder from Aldeburgh, and in the eighteenth century by Mr Perry, who built the seven-storey Blackwall Mast House, where masts could be fitted and timber stored. Poplar always looks and feels as if it was heavily bombed, without any relics of its seventeenth-century shipyards and consisting mainly of large 1930s and 1950s estates. At its heart is St Matthias, which still contains within its mid-Victorian ragstone casing the original chapel of the East India Company, first opened in the early 1650s.

St Matthias
Churchyard

Poplar

The former Board of
Works, opened in 1870.

And this is the old
Chaplain's House, with
the arms of the East India
Company in the pediment.

Robin Hood Gardens

A decision was made to
demolish Robin Hood
Gardens by Margaret
Hodge when Minister for
Culture, supported by the
Commissioners of English
Heritage, in spite of it being
one of the more important
surviving examples of post-
war housing and designed
by Alison and Peter Smithson.
It is still there, with an
eastern-European air of
neglect but full of what look
like architecture students,
retaining its original
sculptural sweep and no more
gloomy – in fact, much less so
– than the rest of Poplar.

Poplar

Balfron Tower

The nearby Balfron Tower
is Ernö Goldfinger's
monumental, if bleak, tower
block, which overlooks the
entrance to the Blackwall
Tunnel. I was told it was
particularly fine in its
relationship to its setting.
It's not quite my style, but
I can see that it's impressive.

St Mary and
St Joseph

The last of my Poplar sights
is the Catholic church of
St Mary and St Joseph,
which is said by Pevsner
to be at odds with the
picturesque surroundings
of the Lansbury estate
('the mannered modernistic
Gothic detail is totally at
odds with the character
of the surroundings'). It is
the work of Adrian Gilbert
Scott, grandson of Sir
Gilbert Scott, younger
brother to Sir Giles Gilbert
Scott and architect of the
Anglican cathedral in Cairo.
It is an effective marrying
of Scandinavian modernist
brickwork with robust French
Gothic massing.

Poplar

ALDGATE

St George's German Lutheran Church /122 /A

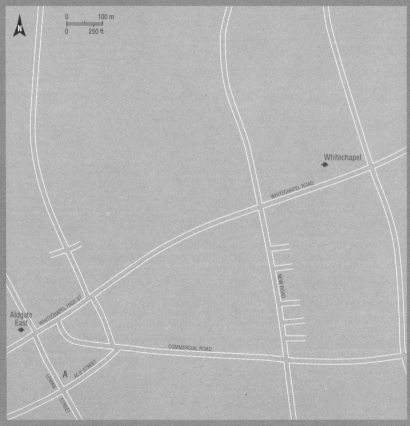

Aldgate & Whitechapel

I'm not sure that **Aldgate** can be described as a neighbourhood. It's in the lee of the City, to which it was once a gateway, with a cattle market just outside the city walls. Now it's a big traffic junction – still marking the gateway to East London – with a couple of useful tube stations: Aldgate (Circle and Metropolitan lines) and Aldgate East (District and Hammersmith & City). The latter is the means of access to the Whitechapel Art Gallery and Brick Lane. Aldgate used to be the home of Bloom's, one of the great East End Jewish restaurants, which closed in 1996. The area now shows signs of new life, with the opening of the Exmouth Coffee Company next door to the Whitechapel Art Gallery, and the Straits Times Kopitiam Coffee Shop opposite. In wandering around it, I am struck by the ambiguity of it as a neighbourhood: forever on the threshold of the City. It was bounded in the eighteenth century by the walls of the City to the north of Bevis Marks and Poor Jury Lane, and intersected by Leadenhall and Fenchurch Streets. As one of my correspondents pointed out, it used to be known as Gardiner's Corner after a large neo-baroque department store at the junction of Whitechapel High Street and the Commercial Road (opposite the tube station) that sold clothes to mariners, from socks to an Admiral's hat. Now the boundary of the City is moving eastwards, with huge new office buildings crowding out the old roundabout.

Aldgate

It is odd and impressive how Petticoat Lane and the Sunday morning market survive, but only just, weaving their way northwards from the tube station nearly to Liverpool Street.

St George's German Lutheran Church

I was wandering past the front door of the old-established Lutheran church on Alie Street and luckily realized that there might be someone able to let me in. It's an extraordinarily pure survival of the German community in eighteenth-century London, who came in search of work (they ran the local sugarhouses) or employment at the Hanoverian court. The church was consecrated on 19 May 1763. It cost £1,802 10s 6d, most of which was provided by Dederich Beckmann, a local sugar refiner and father-in-law of the first pastor. The builder was Joel Johnson who had a workshop nearby, had been involved in the construction of the London Hospital, and is said to have been the architect of the church of St John in Wapping.

WHITECHAPEL

Whitechapel Streets /128
New Road /130 /A
Whitechapel Road /134 /B
Whitechapel Station /136 /C
The London Hospital /138 /D
Working Lads' Institute /138 /E
Brady Street Cemetery /140 /F

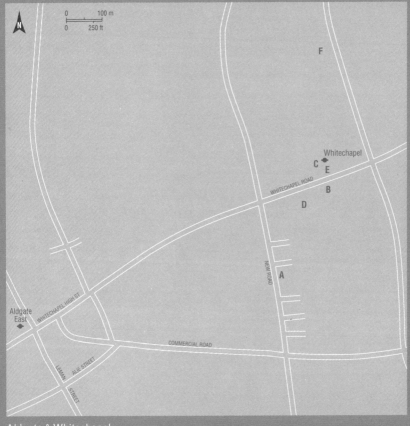

Aldgate & Whitechapel

Whitechapel was already flourishing as a suburb outside the gates of the City in the thirteenth century, and by the early sixteenth century John Stow was able to lament the disappearance of its former beauty and the fact that it had been 'so encroached upon by building of filthy cottages'. By the eighteenth century it was well developed as a meeting place outside the walls of the City, where the main road from Essex landed up, where cattle were driven to abattoirs and where there was a hay market, only closed in 1928, close to the parish church of St Mary Matfelon. It remains densely built, with tightly packed streets around the old London Hospital that has been there since the 1740s. I particularly admire the work that the Spitalfields Trust has done in regenerating the streets off New Road – Turner Street, Walden Street and Varden Street – where the small artisans' houses have been spruced up and gentrified.

Walden Street.

The junction of Turner Street
and Varden Street.

The back of the house at the
junction.

Turner Street.

Varden Street.

New Road

New Road itself has
Gloucester Terrace, with
late eighteenth-century
houses with Coade stone
on the door surrounds.

I liked the wedding door
surround in Parfett Street.

The Whitechapel Bell
Foundry has good
detailing on its façade.

I admire the new Rachel
Whiteread detailing on the
frieze of the Whitechapel
Art Gallery.

And the terracotta ornament
on the façade of the Passmore
Edwards library next door.

Whitechapel Road

In walking to the local post
office under the absurd
delusion that there might still
be a collection on a Sunday,
I noticed how well the façades
of the Whitechapel Road
look now that they have been
cleaned up under a Heritage
Lottery Fund scheme, dating
back from when the road
was planned to be Olympic
Boulevard.

I had never noticed
the fine memorial to
Edward VII, 'ERECTED
FROM SUBSCRIPTIONS
RAISED BY THE JEWISH
INHABITANTS OF EAST
LONDON 1911'.

The old Albion Brewery, once the home of Mann's brown ale, was established in 1808, bought by Blake & Mann in 1818, and run by Mann Crossman & Paulin from 1846 until it amalgamated with Watney Combe Reid in 1958 to become Watney Mann.

Whitechapel

Whitechapel Station

I've always liked Whitechapel
Station, where the District
Line emerges blinking into
the daylight and curves round
to head eastwards towards
West Ham and Upminster,
while below one could
catch the old branch line
of the Metropolitan down to
New Cross, now revitalized
by becoming part of the
London Overground. The
station opened in 1902 and
one used to be able to get the
Whitechapel & Bow Railway
all the way to Southend. It
once had four platforms,
but is now reduced to two,
and it's gradually losing its
character as it is submerged
by the changes required for
Crossrail.

Whitechapel

The London Hospital

London Hospital is not a pretty building, but is unexpectedly reassuring in a medical emergency. One can sneak out for some tandoori chicken at Tayyabs, the best known of the local Indian restaurants, which is nearly impossible to get into in the evening. En route, I spotted the London Hospital's museum with its examples of early medicine chests.

The hat that the Elephant Man wore is surprisingly moving, together with the sackcloth mask that was made to disguise his face.

Working Lads' Institute

As I come out of the London Hospital, my eye is caught by the very faint lettering on the tall building next to the tube. It says, but so faintly as to be scarcely legible, WORKING LADS INSTITUTE, and down below are entrances to rooms that were once a lecture hall and a gymnasium. It goes back to late Victorian philanthropy that launched the Institute at Mansion House in 1876 and opened the building, designed by George Baines, in 1884. It had a library, gymnasium, bank and swimming baths to give boys something to do outside work, and to provide a home for those coming out of gaol. In 1896, it was taken over by the Rev. Thomas Jackson as the headquarters of the Whitechapel Methodist Mission, which continued the good work of helping orphans and destitute lads, sending them to work on farms in Devon.

Gwynne House is a remarkably
well-preserved example of
1930s modernism. It was
designed by Hume Victor Kerr
in 1934, originally as student
accommodation, but now flats.

Brady Street
Cemetery

Brady Street Cemetery is
one of the oldest and largest
of the East End Jewish
cemeteries. Opened in May
1761 in what was then called
Ducking Pond Lane, it's
now sandwiched between
Sainsbury's and the railway
tracks – an inaccessible
piece of empty woodland not
much more than a stone's
throw from the City. It was
due to be redeveloped in the
1980s until Victor Rothschild,
bibliophile and director of the
Think Tank established by
Ted Heath, chose to be buried
next door to his ancestors,
Nathan and Hannah. Access
to the cemetery is strictly
prohibited.

Whitechapel

STEPNEY

Dirty Burger /146 /A
Trinity Green /148 /B
Wickham's Department
Store /150 /C
Spiegelhalter's /150 /C
Bellevue Place /152 /D
Charrington's /152 /E
Stepney Streets /154
A House in Stepney /156
Mile End Road /158
Jubilee Street /160 /F
Stepney Green /160 /G
37, Stepney Green /162 /G
Stepney Green Court /164 /G
Cressy House /166 /H

St Dunstan's, Stepney /170 /J
Stepney City Farm /176 /K
Lady Mico's Almshouses /178 /L
Stepney Meeting Ground /180 /M
King John's Court /180 /N
Withy House /182 /O
Mile End Place /182 /P
The Ocean Estate /184 /Q
Stepney Board School /184 /S
Bancroft Road Public Library /186 /T
Clement Attlee /186 /U
Novo Cemetery /188 /V
Arts Two, Queen Mary /190 /W
Cranbrook Estate /190 /X
Lakeview Estate /192 /Y

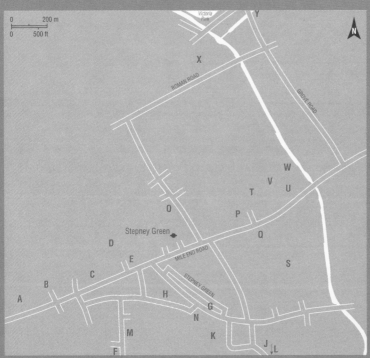

Stepney is by far the oldest part of East London, the first parish east of the City, with a church of Anglo-Saxon origin. St Dunstan and All Saints was already old when Dunstan of Glastonbury replaced the fabric of wood with stone in 952; his name was added to the rest of the saints following his canonization in 1029. By the thirteenth century, Stepney was already a substantial village, stretching down to the river and with a large house on the village green belonging to Henry le Waleys, a merchant who dealt in cloth, hides and most of all wine, and who became Mayor of London. This house belonged in the fifteenth century to Sir Henry Colet, who used it as a country retreat and where his son, John Colet, the humanist and founder of St Paul's School, was rector at a time when it was the richest living in England. By the early eighteenth century, a map by Gascoyne shows a number of houses straggling up from the church alongside the village green, and more houses along the main road in what was described as Mile End Old Town, while the rest of the parish still consisted of fields. In the nineteenth century, it became the classic area of slums, with big tenement blocks, built by Jewish philanthropists, surrounded by close-knit streets. Hitler did much to destroy the sense of community, but post-war development and rehousing did more. We live on the Mile End Road, which doesn't have much to recommend it apart from the broad section outside the old Wickham's Department Store and Genesis Cinema, where there is still a sense of the old drovers' road along which cattle were driven in from the farmland of Essex. To the north of the Mile End Road there is an area of good nineteenth-century terrace housing as well as post-war estates. To the south is Stepney Green, where it is possible to sense the original parish, with grand houses on the east side, including what looks like a manor house.

Dirty Burger

In documenting the rapid
gentrification of Stepney, a
landmark was the opening of
Dirty Burger on the Mile End
Road. It occupies a grand
Edwardian building next to the
Trinity Almshouses. Run by
Soho House, it is an instant
1950s saloon, complete with
light industrial styling, where
you can have flagons of Crate
ale and superior, but not
expensive, burgers.

Stepney

Trinity Green

The almshouses at Trinity
Green were established in
1695 by the will of Captain
Henry Mudd of Ratcliffe
to provide housing for
'28 decayed masters and
commanders of ships or
the widows of such'. There
are model ships, fibreglass
copies of the marble originals,
on the parapet. What is
not recorded is that the
almshouses were saved
as a result of the energies
of C.R. Ashbee, who wrote
The Trinity Hospital in Mile End:
An object lesson in national
history, the first volume of the
Survey of London, published
in 1896 by his Guild of
Handicraft in Bow.

Stepney

Wickham's
Department Store

The old Wickham's
Department Store, designed
as the 'Selfridges of the
East', looks good in the early
morning summer sun. The
original owners gradually
bought up a run of shops
on the north side of the Mile
End Road – all except a small
family clockmakers' called
Spiegelhalter's. When the
Wickhams came to construct a
grand new building in 1927, the
Spiegelhalters refused to sell,
with the result that the grand
Ionic façade is interrupted by a
gap occupied by a single, now
completely derelict, shop. Ian
Nairn loved it and described it
as 'one of the best visual jokes
in London, a perennial triumph
for the little man, the bloke
who won't conform. May he
stay there till the Bomb falls'.

I have seldom seen Wickham's
look so magnificent, its
tower seen from a distance
alongside the line of plane
trees planted in 1910 on Mile
End Waste.

Spiegelhalter's

Now, the bomb may be
about to fall and what little
survives of Spiegelhalter's
replaced by a glass atrium.
It can't be listed because it's
of no obvious architectural
importance (and Wickham's
itself hasn't been listed
despite its significance as
a building type), so there is
pressure instead to persuade
the Tower Hamlets Council
to resist any such plans.

Stepney

Bellevue Place

Bellevue Place, previously
known as Bunghole Alley,
is one of those strange,
secret pockets of the old East
End, where one imagines
artisan engravers might
once have lived. It's tucked in
behind what was Wickham's
Department Store. One
enters by a metal door, which
I expected to be locked, to
find an overgrown cul-de-sac
full of summer flowers.

Charrington's

Living near what was once
one of the main breweries
of Bass Charrington, now a
retail park, I am interested
in the history of the brewery.
Its origins lie in a brewery
in Bethnal Green founded
in the early eighteenth
century by Robert Westfield.
He teamed up with Robert
Moss in 1757 and they
established the original
Anchor Brewery in Mile End.
They then joined forces
with John Charrington, the
son of a vicar. Charrington
was running a brewery in
Islington. Together, they
established Westfield, Moss
& Charrington, becoming
Charrington's after Moss
retired in 1783. John's
brother Henry ran the
brewery from a nearby house
on the Mile End Road. It was
the second largest brewery in
London, a massive operation
of which now only the
adjacent offices, designed
in 1872 by Snooke and Stock,
remain.

Stepney

Stepney Streets

As summer approaches,
I like walking home through
the back streets of Stepney.
There are unexpected pieces
of Bangladeshi decoration.

Even the Corbusian housing
estates look surprisingly
magnificent in the setting sun.

Stepney

A House in Stepney

I was recently asked to talk to third-year students of Queen Mary University about the history of our house. It wasn't easy because so little is known of its history beyond the fact that it belongs to a piece of mid-eighteenth century ribbon development along the Mile End Road which was then, as it is now, the main road out to Bow, Stratford and Essex beyond. At the time, Stepney was still gentrified. Our house occupies part of the site of a larger house, which had a driveway off the Mile End Road and belonged to a crypto-Jacobite MP called Archibald Hutcheson, who had trained as a barrister, was a Fellow of the Royal Society and married a wealthy widow who had previously been married to the Governor of Bombay. He died on 12 August 1740 and his house was sold to a speculative builder called Thomas Andrews, who built three houses in a row, one of which later belonged to Henry Charrington, who ran the local brewery. There were parlours on the ground floor, bedrooms upstairs and a kitchen in the basement. But how many servants were there and which rooms did they occupy? I wish I knew.

Pictures taken on a bleak November day show the way the sun lit up the unrestored wall of our dining room. The wall was left when we restored the house and dates back to the years when it was a Victorian carriage works and possibly earlier to when it was built, and was covered in some form of textile, of which fragments survive round the nails. The photographs on the shelf were taken in Sherbrooke Village in Nova Scotia, where a photographer replicated the technique of Victorian studio photography.

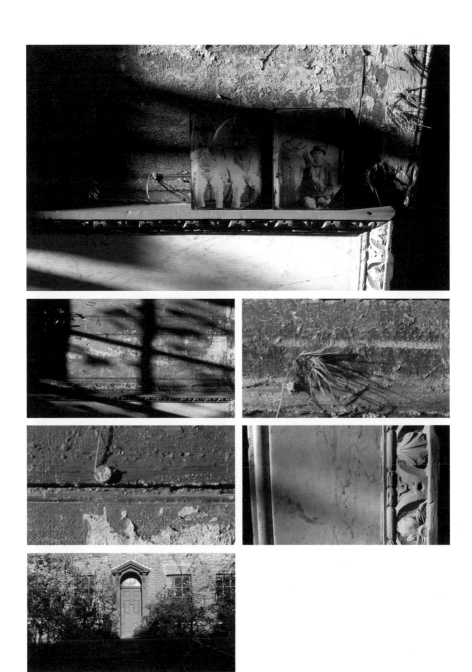

Stepney

Mile End Road

I was wandering past my neighbour's garden and he kindly allowed me to take photographs of his jungle, complete with cenotaph, subtropical vegetation and newly painted front door.

Stepney

Jubilee Street

There are good surviving nineteenth-century terrace houses on Jubilee Street. No. 193 was lived in, according to the 1881 census, by John Abbott, a cowkeeper and owner of Abbott's Yard behind, with a dairy that supplied fresh milk to the City.

In looking up information about Jubilee Street, I was intrigued to discover its revolutionary associations. Lenin spoke on 21 March 1903 in the New Alexandra Hall at a meeting to celebrate the 32nd anniversary of the Paris Commune. The Hall was then leased by an anarchist club. Stalin, then known as Joseph Dzhugashvili, stayed at 77, Jubilee Street in May 1907 when he came to London to attend the 5th RSDLP Congress, after initially lodging in a local doss-house in Fieldgate Street. He was fed toffees by a young boy called Arthur Bacon, who later became a hospital orderly, knew Stalin as Mr Ivanovich, and always remembered his big bushy moustache. Stalin accidentally paid him half a crown to run errands instead of a halfpenny – sixty times the more normal rate. Meanwhile, Lenin was having tea at the workers' club up the street at No. 165. But Lenin preferred to lodge not in Stepney, with his fellow revolutionaries, but in Bloomsbury so as to be close to the British Museum.

Stepney Green

I walked down Stepney Green, thinking (correctly) that it would look good in the morning autumn sun, particularly No. 37, the local Manor House.

Stepney

37, Stepney Green

Central Stepney History Walk,
written by Tom Ridge and
published by the so-called
Central Stepney Regeneration
Board in 1998, has a usefully
concise account of the previous
owners of 37, Stepney Green,
the grandest of the houses
in the neighbourhood. It was
built for Dormer Sheppard,
a London merchant and slave-
owner who twice advertised
for the return of 'a black
Boy named Lewis, about 15
years old, in a Fustian Frock
with Brass Buttons, Leather
Breeches and blue stockings'.
In 1714, it was bought by Lady
Mary Gayer, the widow of
General Sir John Gayer, who
had been Governor of Bombay.
From 1757 to 1763, it was
owned by Laurence Sulivan,
a Director and Chairman of
the East India Company; from
1764 to 1811 by Isaac Lefevre,
a banker and distiller; and,
from 1812 to 1819, by Nicholas
Charrington, proprietor of the
local brewery. It ended up as a
Jewish Home, then The Craft
School, and finally council
offices before being sold to
the Spitalfields Trust in the
mid-1990s. Now it is again a
grand private house.

Stepney

Stepney Green Court

I was walking down Stepney Green past the slightly dour working-class dwellings at the south end beyond the Manor House, when I realized what fine ironwork and stucco detailing they have. They were built in 1895 by Solomon Joseph for the Four Per Cent Industrial Dwellings Company, founded in 1885 by Nathan Rothschild after an enquiry by the United Synagogue into 'spiritual destitution'. Stepney Green court provided 'the industrial classes with commodious and healthy Dwellings at a minimum rent'. Each of the flats had two rooms only and a shared washroom and kitchen, together with a communal club, reading room and baths. The original tenants were mostly Jewish artisans and there was a large synagogue next door, now converted into flats.

One Sunday I went on a casual search for Bert Irvin's studio, which I knew had been on Stepney Green in a Jewish School – I assumed the old Stepney Jewish Primary and Infants School on the south end of the village green that was converted into municipal gardens in 1872. Instead, I found myself inspecting the back façade of Stepney Green Court next door. I'd photographed the ironwork detailing on the street front before, but hadn't previously appreciated the scale of the buildings in two parallel lines off the street.

Stepney

Cressy House

Walking down a road I've
walked down a thousand times
before, not far from our house,
I found myself in a time warp
of 1890s communitarian social
idealism: a well-cared-for
courtyard full of plants, a
small house for the caretaker,
bicycles and beehives. It's
Cressy House, austere on the
outside, designed by Davis &
Emmanuel, architects of the
West London Synagogue,
for the East End Dwellings
Company, with communal
staircases leading off the
internal courtyard.

Stepney

Stepney

St Dunstan's, Stepney

Most weekends I walk
through the churchyard of
St Dunstan's, Stepney, the
ancient church that was at the
heart of the original village.
The church itself is a relic of
a time when Stepney was the
first parish east of London
and Stepney Green was truly
a village green. Dunstan's
original building was replaced
in medieval times, but
was heavily Victorianized,
repaired by Benjamin Ferrey
in the 1840s, gutted by fire in
1901, then damaged during
the war. I was pleased to
discover a monument to John
Charrington, the local brewer.

A rather wonderful piece of
seventeenth-century verse
can be found inside.

The church is bounded
by exceptionally fine
early Victorian ironwork
railings, which somehow
escaped being removed
and repurposed during
the war. An inscription
states that these were the
work of Deeley & Clarke in
Whitechapel, a local iron
foundry based at Buckle
Street. They were installed
in 1844.

St Dunstan's, Stepney

The churchyard of St Dunstan's
is sometimes crisp in the early
morning frost, long shadows
lighting up the pathways,
crocuses and surviving tombs.

Stepney

St Dunstan's, Stepney

A view of the church through
the trees.

One of the tombs inset into
the church's south wall.

The back door.

A detail of the carved
decoration.

And the leaded pipework.

Stepney

Stepney City Farm

I'm not sure that I've ever been to Stepney City Farm previously, other than the Saturday Farmers' Market, except maybe when the children were small to see the pigs. It's an unexpected piece of hippy rusticity next door to where construction workers are currently tunnelling for Crossrail, with geese, donkeys and chickens wandering freely among the lettuces.

Lady Mico's Almshouses

An inscription on the side of the Victorian almshouses to the south of Stepney church reveals that they were the gift of Dame Jane Mico in 1691:

LADY MICO'S ALMSHOUSES FOUNDED AND ENDOWED UNDER THE WILL OF DAME JANE MICO RELICT OF SAMUEL MICO CITIZEN AND MERCER.

Who was she? Her husband, Sir Samuel Mico, grew rich on the profits of the Levant Company and the East India Company, importing silks. He also (surprisingly, since he was a pure Londoner) owned the George Inn in coastal Weymouth. When he died in 1665, he split his estate between his widow, Jane, his nephew, Samuel, the Mercer's Company, and the town of Weymouth, which celebrates his memory every year with lemonade and hot cross buns. Jane, in turn, drew up her will in 1670, leaving money to multitudes of relations, for 'the redemption of Christian slaves in Barbary', as well as for ten poor widows of the City of London who were to be housed in her almshouses. They remained there until 1976, when they were moved to new accommodation in Whitehorse Lane. She also left funds to her nephew, but these went unclaimed because he failed to marry one of his cousins as specified. The funds accrued until they enabled the establishment of a teacher training college in Jamaica.

Stepney

Stepney Meeting Ground

My eye was caught by the fragment of a tomb on the path I take every Sunday morning through the old burial ground of Stepney Meeting House.

The burial ground was opened in 1774 together with almshouses and a charity school. The almshouses were destroyed in the war.

The burial ground is the residue of a Meeting first established in 1644 during the Civil War. A meeting house was built nearby in 1674 by Matthew Mead, the Puritan pastor and former morning lecturer at St Dunstan's (he was the father of Richard Mead, the great doctor and collector).

King John's Court

A gateway survives in among the undergrowth alongside the large Crossrail site just south of Stepney Green. It is all that survives of a chapel that was designed by James Savage and opened in 1831 by Stepney College for the training of Baptist ministers. It occupies the site of a once-moated Tudor mansion which was known as King John's Court, acquired by the Marquis of Worcester in 1597, seized during the Civil War as a headquarters for the parliamentarians, was the birthplace of Richard Mead and is currently being excavated.

There is some lettering on
the pediment that may once
have said 'GOD'.

Withy House

As the years go by, I become
less hostile to the big
Corbusian estates, based on
the Unité d'habitation, which
were put up with such zeal by
the London County Council
in the late 1950s when the
architects' department was
run by Leslie Martin. I'm
more appreciative of their
social ambition, however
misplaced, and their abstract
geometry, played out in
their balconies, particularly
when the sun shines. This
is Withy House on Globe
Road (architect apparently
unknown).

Mile End Place

I called in on Mile End Place
one Christmas morning
– one of those snickets of
artisan housing, backing
on to the Jewish cemetery,
with only trees beyond.

Stepney

The Ocean Estate

The Ocean Estate has a
bad name, but I've always
liked the low-rise houses,
which are well-maintained,
with a great deal of highly
individualistic styling and
a collective atmosphere
redolent of the Homes for
Heroes of 1950s Britain.

Stepney Board School

I took a minor deviation from
my normal Sunday-morning
route and spotted that an
old Board School on the far
side of Shandy Park had been
converted into luxury flats.
It is described in the sales
particulars as 'dating back
to the Second World War',
which shows how much estate
agents know of architectural
history as it so obviously
dates back to the Queen Anne
Revival. It is the surviving
wing of the original Ben
Jonson School, constructed
in 1872 on the Prussian model,
and contained a Cookery
and Laundry Centre, added
in 1895, as well as the local
School Board's divisional
offices.

Stepney

Bancroft Road
Public Library

A long time ago I used to
research local history in
Bancroft Road Public Library.
It's a fine building, designed
in the 1860s as a vestry hall
and converted into a public
library with the help of
funding from the Carnegie
Trust. But it's now looking run
down and, like all the libraries
in Tower Hamlets, has been at
risk of sale (our old library in
Limehouse has been sold as
a restaurant). Let's hope
it survives.

Clement Attlee

I remember when the statue
of Clement Attlee was
placed outside Limehouse
Library. Of course, it could
be regarded – and probably
is – by some as a piece of
reactionary neo-realism,
but I have always thought of
it as a surprisingly convincing
example of modern figurative
sculpture. It's now in the
grounds of Queen Mary
University.

Stepney

Novo Cemetery

As one walks through
the grounds of Queen
Mary University, past the
engineering building and
next to the arts and law
faculties, one finds a large,
well-preserved Jewish burial
ground. It was opened in
1733, next door to Bancroft's
Hospital, and is shown
clearly on Roque's map in the
following decade. Closed for
burials in 1905, the site was
acquired by Queen Mary in
1984, when half the graves
were removed to Brentwood.

Stepney

Arts Two,
Queen Mary

Reading a recent book about
the work of the architectural
practice Wilkinson Eyre
made me realize that not
only are they responsible,
which I knew, for the design
of Arts Two at Queen Mary
University, which houses the
history department with its
ceramic façade designed by
Jacqui Poncelet, but also
for the colourful polyhedral
façade of the School of
Mathematical Sciences.
The screenprinted tiling is
based on the ideas of Roger
Penrose, a visiting professor,
about repeatable and non-
repeatable pattern.

Cranbrook Estate

Just north of the Roman
Road is a modernist estate
with characteristic patterned
façades, punctuated by green
blocks, and with buildings
originally designed on
a figure-of-eight street.
It is a late work by Berthold
Lubetkin, working in
partnership with Francis
Skinner and Douglas Bailey,
both of whom had also worked
for Tecton. Commissioned
by the borough of Bethnal
Green in 1955 after Lubetkin
had retreated to a farm in
Gloucestershire, compulsory
purchase took place in 1957
and the first blocks opened
in 1963.

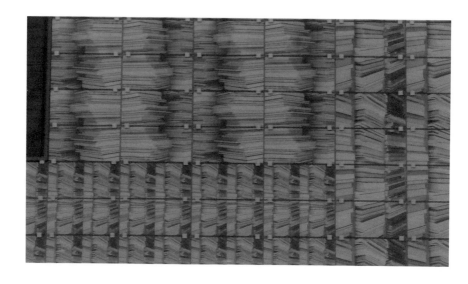

Stepney

Lakeview Estate

Another estate by Lubetkin lies just south of Victoria Park. It has some of the same hallmarks as the nearby Cranbrook Estate, which is visible along the Hertford Union Canal, but Lakeview has distinctive side pavilions that look as if they might be in rural Slovakia.

MILE END

Mile End Park /198 /A
Tredegar Square /202 /B
Tower Hamlets Cemetery /204 /C

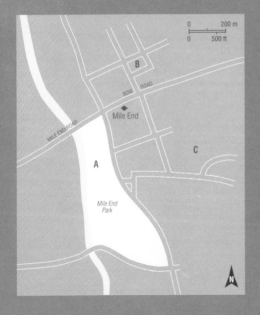

It's not really clear if **Mile End** is a district in its own right, as people who live in what used to be called Mile End Old Town now describe themselves as living in Bow. However, I have kept the memory of its name to describe the area in the vicinity of the underground station, described in 1288 as La Mile Ende, and the Park, which is a lung for the East End. It was originally common land, and was the site of the Peasants' Revolt in 1381, but was already being encroached upon by 'filthy cottages' by the end of the sixteenth century. C.R. Ashbee lived in a large house opposite the station and the Bishop of Stepney used to live on the north side of Tredegar Square. Tredegar Square itself was gentrified in the 1970s, as were the surrounding streets, which has given Bow its cachet, more than the cockney resonance of Bow bells (in the traditional cockney vernacular, 'Bow bells' actually refers to the Wren church of St Mary-le-Bow in the City) or the old village of Bow itself, which lies further east.

Mile End Park

Mile End Park can look
beautiful, with Canary Wharf
shimmering in the distance,
Piers Gough's yellow bridge
gleaming, and canal boats
lined up by the towpath.

The view of Canary Wharf
across the park.

The canal boats.

And the towpath.

The Yellow Bridge, officially
known as 'the Green Bridge'
and unofficially as the
banana bridge, was designed
by Piers Gough, who lives
nearby, with funding from the
Millennium Commission.

Mile End

Tredegar Square

Much the grandest of the
East End squares is Tredegar
Square, just north of the
Mile End tube station. It was
laid out on land belonging
to Sir Charles Morgan of
Tredegar House, a large
Caroline house just outside
Newport, by William King,
an architect-cum-surveyor.
The houses were stuccoed
in the 1830s, giving it a whiff
of the Brighton seafront,
and it was always gentrified
by comparison to the
surrounding neighbourhood.

Nearly as fine are the neighbouring streets; this is Coborn Street.

Coborn Road, previously known as Cut Throat Lane and which once had its own railway station.

Tower Hamlets
Cemetery

Tower Hamlets Cemetery is off
my local map, tucked between
Mile End tube station and the
railway track.

Mile End

BOW

St Mary, Bow Road /210 /A
Bryant & May Factory /212 /B

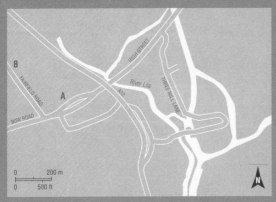

Bow & Bromley-by-Bow

Bow originally grew up as a parish next to the bridge across
the River Lea that was built on the orders of Queen Maud,
the wife of Henry I. It is said to have been shaped like a bow.
It had a nunnery to the south of the bridge and a medieval
parish church which still survives, but only just, half-
underneath the flyover to Stratford. In the eighteenth century,
the Bow porcelain factory was established on the other side
of the river by Edward Heylyn and an Irish painter, Thomas
Frye; it supplied cheaper ware than Chelsea. In 1800, Bow was
still no more than a village, clustered round the church. But by
1900, it had been engulfed by London and was the site of small
factories that took advantage of the river, manufacturing soap,
hemp and rubber, as well as the great Bryant & May match
factory just north of the church on Fairfield Road. Now any
sense of it being a coherent village has been destroyed – and
the old medieval church sits within a roundabout on a spur
of the A11.

St Mary, Bow Road

I went to see St Mary, Bow
Road, but at a bad time
as there was a service –
with a surprisingly large
congregation, considering
the church sits in the middle
of a roundabout. Some of it
at least is fourteenth century,
but the tower looks younger,
partly because it was rebuilt
after the war. The church
owes its preservation to the
failure of numerous plans to
rebuild it in the nineteenth
century, and to C.R. Ashbee,
who oversaw a conservative
restoration in the 1890s.

The ceiling.

The west window, which
looks fungoid.

Bow

Bryant &
May Factory

I wandered into the old
Bryant & May match factory,
scene of the strike in 1888
and subject of an essay
by Patrick Wright in *A
Journey Through Ruins*.
William Bryant and Francis
May started importing
Swedish matches in 1850.
In 1855 they acquired a
patent to manufacture
safety matches from red
phosphorus and potassium,
and in 1861 they opened the
Fairfield Works, a massive
factory, rather German in
character with its red and
black brick. The workers
were first radicalized in
1871 in protest against the
planned imposition of a tax
on matches, and again went
on strike in 1888, led by the
theosophist Annie Besant.
It's all quiet now after being
converted into apartments
in 1987.

East London

BROMLEY-BY-BOW

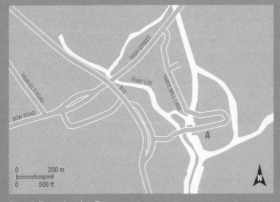

Bow & Bromley-by-Bow

Bromley-by-Bow is now not much more than a ghost town, its name retained in the old High Street and as a stop on the District Line. It was once the site of the Old Palace of Bromley and, to the south, Bromley Hall; but Bromley Hall already had a calico printing works attached to it by 1799, while the Old Palace in St Leonard's Street was demolished in 1894 to create a Board School, its Jacobean panelling removed to the V&A. The last vestiges of the parish church, which was the Lady Chapel of the old convent, were levelled to make way for the approach road to the Blackwall Tunnel.

Three Mills

Three Mills is an unexpected
piece of industrial archaeology,
next to Tesco in Bromley-
by-Bow. As mills, they were
first established before the
dissolution of the monasteries
to supply grain to the bakeries
of Stratford-atte-Bow. They
were later acquired in 1727
by three Huguenots to distil
gin. The date 1776 survives on
the façade, when the mill was
rebuilt for Daniel Bisson, one of
the three, but most of the current
structure – where it is not a
facsimile by the conservation
architect Julian Harrap – dates
to 1802.

STRATFORD

Queen Elizabeth Olympic Park /224 /A
Abbey Mills Pumping Station /230 /B

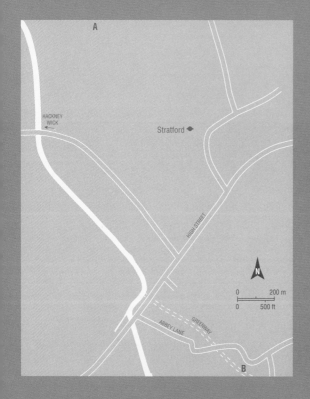

Stratford is changing fast, owing to the Olympics. In the eighteenth century it was said by Daniel Defoe to be full of 'hansom large houses', built as the country houses and retirement homes of City folk, and it became the site of the Bow porcelain works, opened by Edward Heylyn and Thomas Frye and known as 'New Canton'. But in the nineteenth century it became solidly and toughly working class, the site of railway works. Michael Heseltine saw it as a prime site for urban development, and London's successful Olympic bid has led to a radical transformation of the area – not just the creation of the Olympic Park, but new housing along the main road into Stratford.

Queen Elizabeth Olympic Park

The Olympic Park is a mistake: too much clutter and not enough park. However, Anish Kapoor's ArcelorMittal Orbit looks better close up, like an escaped triffid.

The view from the top of
the ArcelorMittal tower
is spectacular.

Queen Elizabeth Olympic Park

Zaha Hadid's Aquatics
Centre is impressive,
like a sculptural sun visor.

Queen Elizabeth
Olympic Park

Best of all was the terrine
and coriander hummus at
the Hackney Pearl, now
closed, over the bridge in
Hackney Wick.

Abbey Mills
Pumping Station

I walked out to Sir Joseph
Bazalgette's Abbey Mills
Pumping Station by way of
the Greenway path, which
stretches all the way from
Victoria Park to Plaistow and
on to Beckton. Beginning
across a bridge over the
Hertford Union canal, it's
quite a romantic walk – made
possible by sewage: the
Greenway runs along the top
of the Northern Outfall Sewer.

There are views across
the wasteland towards
Canary Wharf.

Then, past Stratford, the
'Cathedral of Sewage' comes
into view.

Abbey Mills
Pumping Station

Brendan Finucane very kindly
arranged for us to have a
private tour of Abbey Mills
Pumping Station, which
stands proud in the valley
of the River Lea on the site
of a monastic water mill.
It's an amazing building,
with so much decorative
care and Byzantine and
Gothic detail lavished on
Sir Joseph Bazalgette's
powerhouse of engineering.
Inside is full of hand dials
and maps of London's
sewers and Piranesian
vistas, down to the big pipes
that transport London's
sewage out to Beckton, all of
it constructed after the Great
Stink of 1858.

It's a fine structure, with its
polychromatic arched windows
and spiky Russian lantern.

The grand entrance.

Details of the decorative carving.

The great interior.

The 1930s pumps.

The map of London's sewers.
The dials.
And, last, the tool kit.

This is the modern equivalent,
by Allies and Morrison.

Stratford

SPITALFIELDS

The Bishopsgate
Institute /244 /A

Verde & Company /244 /B

London Fruit &
Wool Exchange /246 /C

Christ Church,
Spitalfields /248 /D

Norton Folgate
Almshouses /252 /E

Fournier Street /254 /F

31 Fournier Street /254 /F

Princelet Street /258 /G

11 Princelet Street /260 /G

Gallery SO /262 /H

Libreria /262 /J

Norton Folgate /264 /K

Elder Street /266 /L

Truman Hanbury Buxton
& Company /268 /M

Cereal Killer Cafe /270 /N

Victoria Cottages /272 /O

St Anne's, Underwood
Road /272 /P

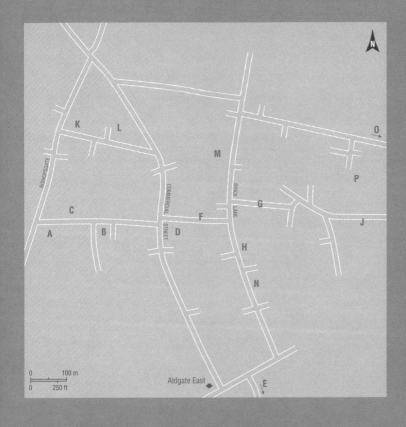

Spitalfields is at the heart of what was the original East End, close to the City and always connected to it, but an area of silkweaving in the early eighteenth century, when the rich weavers lived in houses behind the church and the poorer ones worked from home in the attics and back yards of the houses round about. In the nineteenth century, the silk industry declined and the area became poorer, but still with fine, well-preserved eighteenth-century houses. In the 1960s, old and dilapidated Georgian houses surrounded the Victorian fruit and vegetable market. Raphael Samuel lived in 19, Elder Street and, in an essay in *The Saving of Spitalfields*, describes how 'The Georgian streets – or "Queen Anne Houses" as they were then generally called – had been preserved by their poverty from improvement. There was peeling stucco in the doorways and fanlights crusted over with dust, but when one went inside a house the panelling was intact, the original floor boards were still in place, and the window panes, as often as not, filled with antique glass'. In the 1970s, the middle-class invasion began. Mariga Guinness, an alcoholic German princess with a taste for building conservation, bought a house in Elder Street and Anna Skrine, an Anglo-Irishwoman, held court in Wilkes Street. Mark Girouard, Colin Amery and Dan Cruickshank campaigned to save Elder Street. The Spitalfields Trust was established in 1977. By the 1980s, the New Georgians were in command. Spitalfields can sometimes feel a bit too New England for my taste. But it is inescapably a model of effective urban regeneration and is now the epicentre of young and fashionable London.

Spitalfields

The south façade of the
church, seen from the
churchyard.

The market.

Christ Church, majestic as ever, presides over the market and surrounding streets.

Shop signs.

Kippers for breakfast at St. John Bread and Wine.

Spitalfields

On Crispin Street, next door to
what was Tracey Emin's shop,
there's the Convent of the
Sisters of Mercy, with separate
entrances for men and women.

Artillery Lane has No. 56,
one of the best preserved
mid-eighteenth-century shop
fronts, built for Francis Rybot,
a silk merchant, and now the
art gallery Raven Row.

Here's Fournier Street.

And Wilkes Street.

The convent and Artillery Lane.

A detail of Anna Maria Garthwaite's house in Princelet Street. She did wonderful watercolour drawings for the silk industry from the 1720s to 1756.

The Bishopsgate Institute

The Bishopsgate Institute
was opened in 1895 to provide
enlightenment to the East
End; it was designed by
Charles Harrison Townsend,
later architect of the
Whitechapel Art Gallery
and the Horniman Museum
too. It's got fine, quite free
art nouveau detailing on the
terracotta entrance façade.

Verde & Company

No visit to Spitalfields is
complete without a trip to
Verde & Company, run by
Harvey Cabaniss, a supplier
of Pierre Marcolini chocolates
– the best chocolates in the
world – as well as of assorted
baskets, knick-knacks, silver
teapots and Yorkshire Parkin.

Spitalfields

London Fruit &
Wool Exchange

It's odd how one can
think one knows a London
neighbourhood and then
discover that an enormous
chunk of it has disappeared
for redevelopment. This
is true of the massive site
immediately opposite
Spitalfields Market that was
previously a multi-storey
car park (I remember that)
and before that the London
Fruit & Wool Exchange, a not
especially distinguished 1920s
classical building that opened
in 1929 for fruit and vegetable
auctions. The façade facing
Brushfield Street has been
kept and looks faintly surreal,
propped up on the other side
of the vacant building site,
which is being redeveloped
by Rab Bennetts.

Spitalfields

Christ Church,
Spitalfields

Owen Hopkins's short
monograph *From the
Shadows: The Architecture
and Afterlife of Nicholas
Hawksmoor* made me look
afresh at Christ Church,
Spitalfields, in the light of
his very clear account of
the way that Hawksmoor
was influenced by the
interest of his ecclesiastical
contemporaries in the
churches of the Primitive
Christians. This may
have given Hawksmoor
some of his characteristics
of bold, unornamented,
structural clarity.

East London

Spitalfields

Spitalfields

Norton Folgate
Almshouses

While thinking about the pros
and cons of the development
of Norton Folgate, I noticed
that the small group of
Victorian almshouses
in Puma Court, just off
Commercial Road, is called
Norton Folgate Almshouses.
As the inscription reveals,
they replace an earlier
group of almshouses, built
in 1728 but demolished to
create 'The New Street' –
presumably the north half
of Commercial Street laid
out by James Pennethorne
in the 1850s to connect the
docks to Great Eastern Street.

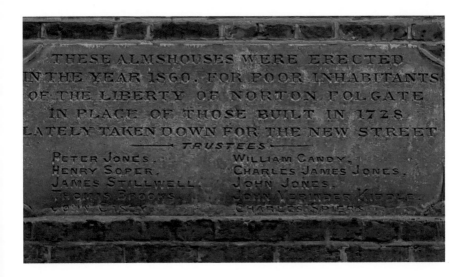

The new almshouses were
designed by T.E. Knightley
and opened in 1860.

Fournier Street

I can't resist photographing Fournier Street's beautiful, still-surviving door surrounds, and remembering that this part of Spitalfields, now as lush and prosperous as a New England village, wasn't necessarily going to survive forty years ago.

31 Fournier Street

I was tipped off that 31 Fournier Street had a wonderful exhibition of textile designs. What I wasn't told is that the house itself is an amazing survival of old Spitalfields. Its original panelling was discovered under plasterboard by Rodney Archer when he bought the house in 1980 off an Indian taxi firm.

The house backs onto workshops and yards, including the profile of Worrall House, by Samuel Worrall, the original builder of Fournier Street.

The overdoor and window
surround as seen from the
street.

31 Fournier Street

Upstairs was the grandest
of the rooms, complete
with a fireplace that Rodney
rescued from Oscar Wilde's
house in Tite Street.

This is the street where Anna
Maria Garthwaite lived and
created her beautiful textile
designs, which she tailored
according to the season.

And these are details from
further down the street.

Anna Maria Garthwaite's
house.

And the house next door.

11 Princelet Street

I had never previously
walked past Chris Dyson's
architectural practice in
Princelet Street when it
was closed, so had not had
an opportunity to admire
its fine shop lettering, nor
its fire insurance plaques
(first introduced by Sun Fire
Office in 1710), nor the poster
recording its history.

Gallery SO

Gallery SO, the jewellery
gallery sandwiched among
the many Indian restaurants
for which Brick Lane is
famous, is open on the first
Thursday of the month.

Libreria

We heard about Libreria
from the man who made the
cocktails at its opening.
It's the new, über-trendy
bookshop in Hanbury Street
with a mirrored black ceiling
and yellow, packing-case
shelves and stock that is
categorized according to
unconventional subject
matter rather than traditional
subject headings. They don't
allow wi-fi and photography is
banned, so the only way I can
record it is by a picture of one
of its paper bags.

Norton Folgate

I managed to miss out on the arguments surrounding the redevelopment of Norton Folgate, an area of semi-derelict warehouses on the edge of Spitalfields. So, on a sunny, late December morning, I decided to investigate. Blossom Street is an unexpected cobbled street leading to the north from Dennis Severs' House in Folgate Street, and is lined on its eastern side by a series of surviving, well-preserved but currently unused industrial warehouses. The City and Bishopsgate are within spitting distance. It's easy to see the development potential: another big office block. But equally easy to see why the development has been resisted and alternative plans put forward for the renovation of the warehouses.

I was subsequently drawn, without particular intention, into the controversy surrounding the development. Rather than the City developing the properties themselves through their architecture and planning department, they are doing it in conjunction with British Land. What is unusual is that, nearly adjacent to the old industrial warehouses, relics of the trading roots at the fringes of the City, are the original eighteenth-century houses of Elder Street, one of the most

important historic streets in Spitalfields. An alternative plan for the development of the neighbourhood that has been drawn up by Burrell Foley Fischer respects its original mixed character. The plans drawn up by British Land were rejected by Tower Hamlets, but have now been passed by former London mayor Boris Johnson over the heads of local planning. It's a battle between two forms of development, one monolithic and corporate and the other low-rise and conservationist. The battle is now lost. The paradox is that conservationism is almost certainly better at preserving the long-term prosperity and energy of the City as an engine of economic growth.

These are the warehouses.

Elder Street

In order to understand the
nature of the argument
surrounding the development
of Norton Folgate, it is
important to see it in the
context of Elder Street, one
of the best of the surviving
Spitalfields streets, where the
artist Mark Gertler lived, and
later Raphael Samuel and now
Dan Cruickshank. The City
looms nearby. But there is
still a domestic presence
resisting the incursion.

Truman Hanbury
Buxton & Company

The origins of this brewery go back to 1666 when Thomas Bucknall established a brewhouse on 'Lolsworth Field at Spittlehope'. The business was taken over in 1694 by Joseph Truman. His son Benjamin became a partner in 1722 and helped build up production, particularly of porter, such that they were producing 83,000 barrels a year in 1766 (not just porter, but also three types of stout and a mild ale). Benjamin became a country gentleman with an estate in Hertfordshire, and was painted by Gainsborough, appointed High Sheriff, and knighted by George III. In 1775, he wrote his credo on a page of the company accounts: 'There can be no other way of raising a great Fortune but by carrying on an Extensive Trade. I must tell you Young Man, this is not to be obtained without Spirrit and great Application'. Following his death in 1780, the Quaker Hanburys bought into the firm. Sampson Hanbury, whose father Osgood was a banker and mother Mary a Lloyd (of the banking family), is said to have been a brilliant businessman, installing a steam engine in the factory in 1805, and producing 200,000 barrels by 1820. He bought a country estate at Poles in Hertfordshire in 1800. In 1808, his nephew Thomas Buxton joined the firm. He reformed its management, encouraged literacy in the workforce and in 1818 entered parliament as MP for Weymouth.

A black eagle, the sign of the brewery.

The sign of The Jolly Butchers up the road, one of many pubs now closed.

Cereal Killer Cafe

I had read about the shop in Brick Lane that sells nothing but breakfast cereals and thought that it was no more than a modern urban myth until I passed it, looked through the window, and saw people enjoying their morning bowlfuls. I was told recently that Kellogg's cornflakes were invented by religious fundamentalists to suppress the libido, and have discovered to my amazement that this is true: John Harvey Kellogg was a virulent anti-masturbator. But I can't see why anyone would want to masturbate at breakfast.

Victoria Cottages

I've often passed, but never
investigated, the little run
of Victorian cottages off
Deal Street. They were
designed in 1864 for the
Metropolitan Association
for Improving the Dwellings
of the Industrious Classes
(founded 1841). They are a
relic of the low-rise, more
community-oriented, pre-war
East End, as documented by
Young and Willmott in their
very influential 1957 study
*Family and Kinship in East
London.*

St Anne's,
Underwood Road

The Roman Catholic church
of St Anne's was designed in
the 1850s by Gilbert Blount,
a pupil of Pugin, to bring
Catholicism to the Irish
poor who had moved to East
London as labourers after the
potato famine. The church
and adjacent presbytery, both
built in Kentish ragstone, were
in the heart of what was Mile
End New Town and are now
lost amidst an area of flatlands
created by urban clearance
and bombing, next door to
Spitalfields' urban farm.

The front door of the
presbytery.

The church door.

Here is a boss.

And a pinnacle.

SHOREDITCH

Shoreditch Town Hall /278 /A
Wells & Company /280 /B
Mast Brothers /280 /C
Boundary Estate /282 /D
Leila's /282 /E

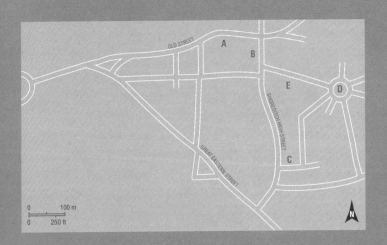

Shoreditch is today the heart of the fashionable East End. It was once the home of the London furniture trade, with large warehouses on Curtain Road and the old tram station nearby. In 1985 Sheridan Coakley opened SCP, a furniture shop stocking reproductions of pieces from the Modern Movement and new designs by Matthew Hilton and Jasper Morrison, and small art galleries began to open nearby. During the 1990s, the Bricklayer's Arms on Charlotte Road was a gathering place for the Young British Artists, and Joshua Compston opened his Factual Nonsense Gallery. Apostrophe opened on Great Eastern Street, the first of a multitude of coffee shops. In 2000, the Prince of Wales opened premises for several of the organizations under his Prince's Trust umbrella in a converted warehouse on Curtain Road. Now, Shoreditch is packed at night, having many clubs and restaurants, including the Clove Club in the old Town Hall, the Rivington Grill in Rivington Street and Hix at the Tramshed.

What struck me as I walked from St. John Bread and Wine up to the Old Street roundabout was the extreme rapidity of the process of urban change: the number of large vacant sites occupying spaces of buildings that were not especially memorable, but have left a large hole now that they are gone. London, and most especially the East End, has benefited from a process of rapid urban improvement and change, first begun long ago under the London Docklands Development Corporation. But it's the speed of it that is disturbing, and the way big new office and apartment buildings damage the ecology of mixed neighbourhoods. Artists move in. Then small fashion boutiques. Then they are ousted by the big chains. Now there's a branch of J.Crew in Redchurch Street. It happened long ago in Chelsea. Now it's happening in Shoreditch.

Shoreditch Town Hall

I normally only see Shoreditch Town Hall late at night, when it is mobbed by teenagers, but I have realized how grand it is and how fine some of its detailing. It was designed by a little-known architect, Caesar Augustus Long, in 1866.

Shoreditch

Wells & Company

Wells & Company was the
old commercial ironmongers
opposite St Leonard's,
Shoreditch. It was built in
1877 for Edward Wells &
Company, which sold stoves,
gutters, pipes and decorative
ironwork to the building
trades. The building,
designed by Fowler & Hill,
is part-Gothic, part-Moorish,
with a surviving mosaic
inscription, 'Wells &
Company Commercial Iron
Works', in spite of the fact
that it ceased trading in 1895
and became a bank.

Mast Brothers

I was once sent some very
delicious chocolate bars
from Williamsburg in New
York. Their makers, Mast
Brothers, have opened a
gigantic chocolate emporium
on Redchurch Street, where
it is possible to not only
buy their chocolate bars
(at a steep price), but also
see the great vats of boiling
chocolate.

Shoreditch

Boundary Estate

The Boundary Estate was built
in the 1890s by the London
County Council as a way of
clearing out the Old Nichol,
a largely criminal district that
was the subject of Arthur
Morrison's *A Child of the Jago*,
published in 1896, and Raphael
Samuel's classic *East End
Underworld*. It was the first
big estate designed by the
Working Classes branch of the
Architects' Department at the
LCC and has blocks designed
by different architects, all of
which are centred on Arnold
Circus and its bandstand.
Look at the quality of some of
its Arts-and-Crafts detailing,
including the lettering.

Leila's

I like shopping in Leila's
in Calvert Avenue, which is
a good source of almonds,
cheese and organic
vegetables.

East London

Shoreditch

BETHNAL GREEN

St Matthew's, Bethnal Green /288 /A
St Peter's, Bethnal Green /290 /B
Keeling House /292 /C
Hackney Road /294 /D
Blue House /296 /E
Ye Olde Axe /298 /F
Bethnal Green Library /300 /G
Paradise Row /300 /H
V&A Museum of Childhood /301 /J
Netteswell House /302 /K
York Hall and Baths /302 /L
Bethnal Green Town Hall /304 /M
St John on Bethnal Green /306 /N

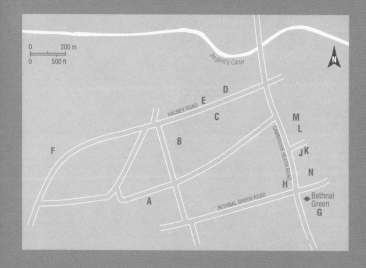

There was once a village green at **Bethnal Green**, with
an Elizabethan house lived in by Sir William Ryder, who
entertained Samuel Pepys with wine and strawberries.
It's hard to believe that it was once an area of market
gardening and silk weaving. In the nineteenth century it
was known for its slums, dominated by solid, back-to-back
working-class housing. Like Stepney, it suffered from
bombing and subsequent redevelopment. My brother bought
a house in Bethnal Green on Quilter Street, just south of
Jesus Green. He was a friend of Richard Naylor, who was
trained as an architect and bought Jones the Dairy in Ezra
Street, just off Columbia Road, which he turned into a
New-Wave, old-fashioned food shop, stocking English cheese
and tea. So I've watched the gradual transformation of
Columbia Road, with its traditional Sunday morning flower
market, now packed on Sundays and with small, smart
boutiques of every kind.

St Matthew's,
Bethnal Green

St Matthew's, the parish
church, was originally
intended to be one of the
Fifty Churches designed
by Hawksmoor. But the
parishioners objected to
the cost and the Rector of
Stepney didn't want to lose
his income from tithes.
So instead, a more modest
church was commissioned
from George Dance the Elder.
Work started in 1743, but
funds were inadequate.
An Act of Parliament
provided funds on the
grounds of the 'dissoluteness
of morals and a disregard for
religion, too apparent in the
younger and poorer sort'.
In the 1850s the interior was
destroyed by fire; then again
in 1940, this time by Hitler.
It was reconstructed in the
1950s by Anthony Lewis of
Tapper & Lewis, with work
commissioned from young
artists. It's a good example
of 1950s ecclesiasticism.

The screen by Peter Snow.

Bethnal Green

St Peter's,
Bethnal Green

St Peter's, Bethnal Green,
is unexpectedly rustic, as
if lost down a leafy, Norfolk
lane, not surrounded by
tough housing estates. It was
designed by Lewis Vulliamy
for Bishop Blomfield and
built in knapped flint and
stock brick.

The vicarage, also by Vulliamy.

The churchyard.

Keeling House

I was only shown Keeling House recently: a muscular and ingeniously geometric early example of work by Denys Lasdun, when he was working for Fry, Drew, Drake & Lasdun in the mid-1950s. It's more purely architectural than the standard LCC blocks, still surrounded by what would have been regarded as Victorian slum housing, now being done up, as Keeling House itself has been.

Bethnal Green

Hackney Road

Pevsner is dismissive of
Hackney Road, but it has good
examples of early Victorian
terrace housing on the north
side – surprisingly grand for
the neighbourhood, which
at the time was beginning
its slide into slumdom.

It shows all the signs of being
gentrified, with new cafés at every
street corner. I liked the decoration
on the old doctor's surgery.

Bethnal Green

Blue House

The nicely jokey Blue
House was designed by
Sean Griffiths of the
now-deceased FAT for
himself, paying homage
to Bob Venturi. It's in
Garner Street, just off
the Hackney Road.

There's a magnificent piece of
surviving industrial lettering
incised into a side wall nearby.

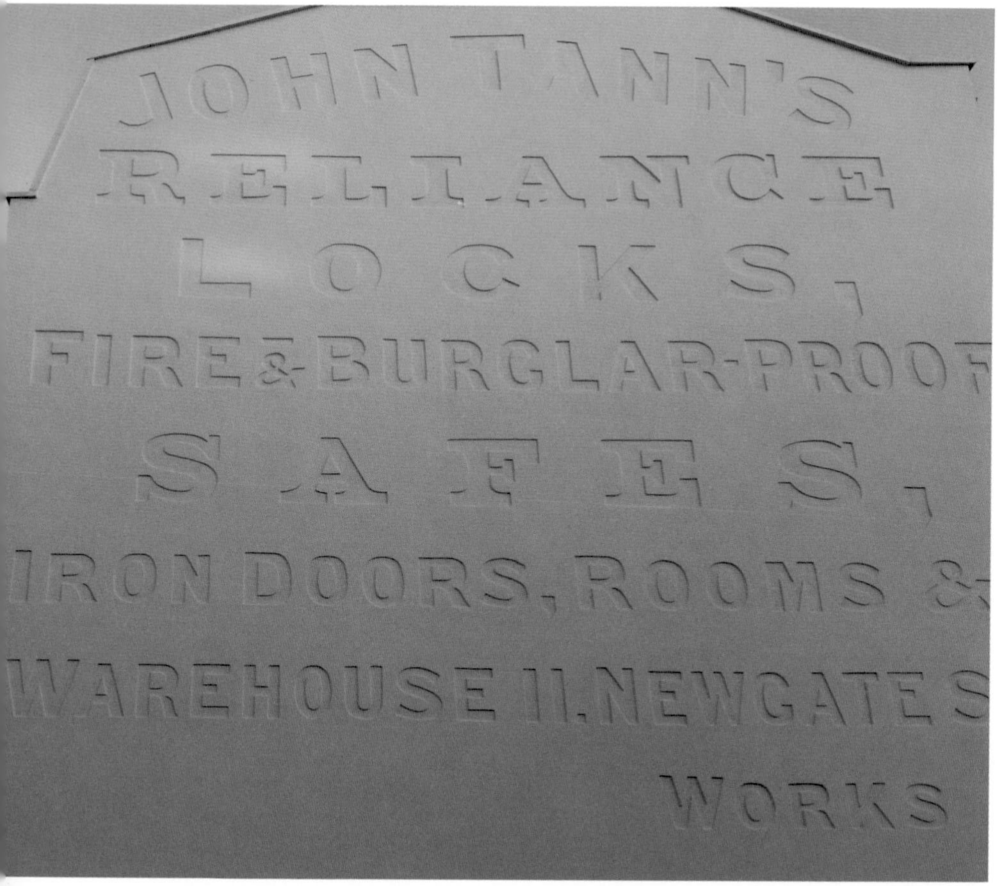

JOHN TANN'S
RELIANCE
LOCKS,
FIRE & BURGLAR-PROOF
SAFES,
IRON DOORS, ROOMS &
WAREHOUSE II, NEWGATE S
WORKS

Bethnal Green

Ye Olde Axe

At the lower end of the
Hackney Road, where it
meets Shoreditch, there
is what I thought was a
deserted pub but turns
out to be a striptease joint,
called Ye Olde Axe. It looks
as if it belongs in the Wild
West, with its turret and
pub sign swinging in
the wind, but has good
terracotta lettering and
very fine capitals.

Bethnal Green

Bethnal Green Library

Bethnal Green Library is a fine piece of municipal socialism, originally built in the 1890s as a wing of the local lunatic asylum and adapted in the 1920s by the Borough Engineer as a library, with bas-reliefs of Charles Darwin, Karl Marx, William Morris and Richard Wagner, as selected by the Town Council, which was part Communist at the time.

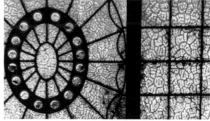

Paradise Row

Just north of the tube station is Paradise Row, a survivor of the original Bethnal Green; a fine street of artisan houses, one of which was lived in by Daniel Mendoza, the great Jewish boxer who was once champion of England.

V&A Museum
of Childhood

I've always liked Bethnal
Green's Museum of
Childhood, now with its new
decorated entrance façade
by Caruso St John. The
building itself was 'designed'
– not really designed, but
constructed – by James
Wild, who also designed
Christ Church, Streatham,
was retained as 'an expert
on Arabian art' at the South
Kensington Museum, and
ended his career as curator
of the Soane Museum.

Around the side of the
museum, a series of mosaic
panels shows the arts and
industries. The panels
were executed by the
students of the National Art
Training Schools under the
supervision of Frank Moody.

Netteswell House

I wish we had been able to
afford to buy Netteswell
House when it was sold
by the V&A for what now
seems like a song in the late
1980s. I don't think I quite
appreciated its significance
as a relic of sixteenth-
century Bethnal Green, when
the ground was leased by
Sir Ralph Warren, a former
Lord Mayor. The house itself
is part mid-seventeenth
century, part 1705, and
part 1862.

York Hall and Baths

Just north of the Bethnal
Green Museum is the York
Hall and Baths, where the
citizens of Bethnal Green
come to box, wash their
laundry and take a Turkish
bath.

Bethnal Green

Bethnal Green
Town Hall

I had read somewhere that the back elevation of the recently renovated Bethnal Green Town Hall is one of the top ten pieces of new architecture in London. I was intrigued, as I hadn't registered this elevation (one enters on the opposite side). It's a fine, aluminium, surreal sheath designed by Michel da Costa Gonçalves and Nathalie Rozencwajg of the architectural practice RARE.

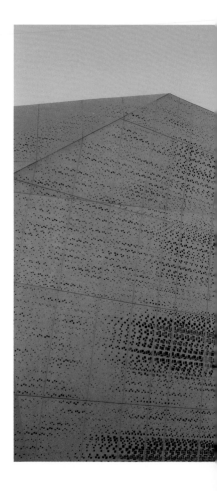

I'm not sure it makes my top ten, but it did encourage me to admire the fine Edwardian façade by Percy Robinson and W. Alban Jones, and the sculpture by Henry Poole that shows the Municipality of Bethnal Green protecting the fruits of local industry.

Bethnal Green

St John on Bethnal Green

A trip to the local polling station gave me a chance to document the church tower of St John on Bethnal Green, designed by Sir John Soane in 1826 for the Commissioners of the 1818 Church Building Act at more or less the same time that he was designing St Peter's, Walworth and Holy Trinity, Marylebone. It's the standard model of a Commissioners' church: a big, barn-like interior to maximize the number of pews; ornament restricted to the church tower, which is characteristic of Soane, with a small 'pepper pot' adornment that was originally planned to be much higher.

Bethnal Green

HOXTON

Kingsland Road /312 /A

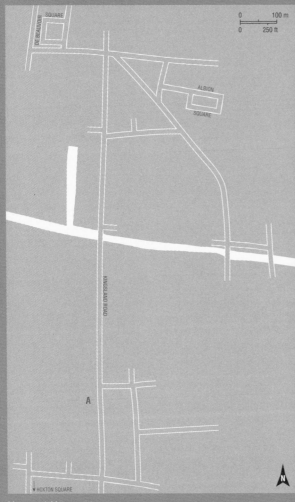

Hoxton & Haggerston

Hoxton is the area north of Shoreditch, less obviously fashionable than its southern neighbour, apart from Hoxton Square, previously the site of White Cube gallery. In the sixteenth century, there were manor houses in Hoxton, where Catholics, including Thomas Tresham, came to enjoy the country air; but Hoxton House was turned into a lunatic asylum in the eighteenth century, and in the nineteenth century the area was wholly working class, described by Charles Booth as having 'a considerable admixture of the very poor and vicious'. Indeed, Mary Wollstonecraft was born in Hoxton, and so were the notorious Kray brothers.

Kingsland Road

I went on a Saturday morning
mooch round Hoxton, having
been told during the week
how trendy the Kingsland
Road now is. All I could find
on the Kingsland Road was
some nice detailing.

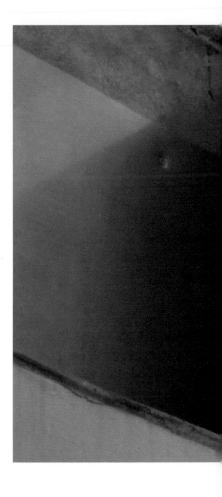

Hoxton

HAGGERSTON

Albion Square /318 /A
De Beauvoir Estate /318 /B
Geffrye Museum /320 /C
Christ Apostolic Church Bethel /322 /D
Kingsland Road /324 /E
St Chad's, Dunloe Street /324 /F

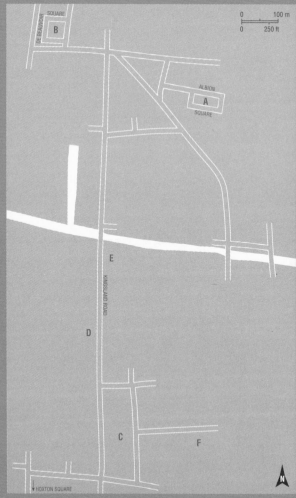

Hoxton & Haggerston

I don't find it easy to tell the difference between Hoxton and **Haggerston**, but they are different wards in the Borough of Hackney and different stops on the new Overground, which has opened up this area of town, connecting it to a grand circular tour of outer London. It was first mentioned in the Domesday Book as 'Hergotestane' and is shown on John Roque's great eighteenth-century map of London as 'Agostone'. In the nineteenth century, it was an area of light industry and furniture-making, with factories alongside the Regent's Canal. These factories have been turned into artists' studios, with a high concentration of studios and smaller avant-garde galleries in Vyner Street and Wadeson Street off the Kingsland Road.

Albion Square and De Beauvoir Estate

I had never been to Albion Square, laid out in the 1840s by Islip Odell, a brick-maker, and was surprised and impressed by its stateliness and its sense of municipal improvement, with drinking fountains and public gardens.

Beyond is the De Beauvoir estate, named after its original owner, the Rev. Peter Beauvoir, and laid out by William Rhodes to designs supplied by James Burton, father of Decimus and designer with Nash of the houses round Regent's Park. This must explain the generosity in the layout of the streets and the quality of some of the detailing. These are examples of the houses in Northchurch Road and Southgate Grove beyond.

A second phase of building took place during the 1840s after Richard Benyon De Beauvoir had inherited the estate. The Jacobethan houses in De Beauvoir Square itself are attributed in *From Tower to Tower Block: The Buildings of Hackney* to Robert Lewis Roumieu and Alexander Dick Gough.

I ended up looking at
Haggerston School, a piece
of 1960s utopianism, designed
by Ernö Goldfinger in 1964.

Haggerston

Geffrye Museum

It's a pleasure walking
past the Geffrye Museum
and seeing how the crisp
November sun lights up
the space in front of the
early eighteenth-century
almshouses. They were
built out of a bequest from
Sir Robert Geffrye, a big
wheel in the Ironmongers'
Company, appointed Sheriff
in 1674 and elected Lord
Mayor in 1684. He died in
1703, leaving the residue
of his estate to be used
to construct fourteen
almshouses, with a chapel
in the middle and a statue
commemorating the founder.

Haggerston

Haggerston

Kingsland Road

The other building that impresses on the Kingsland Road is the one which used to be the Shoreditch and Haggerston Public Library, now apparently apartments, but still a monument to late Victorian spirited baroque. Originally designed as a private house, it was adapted into a public library by Richard J. Lovell (who trained at the Royal Academy) in 1893. It's also a monument to the philanthropy of John Passmore Edwards, the great Cornish journalist, reformer, proprietor and champion of the working classes – it was the second of the libraries that he funded, after Whitechapel the year before.

St Chad's,
Dunloe Street

St Chad's is a large barn-like church designed by James Brooks on a street just behind Haggerston School. Brooks became a student at the Royal Academy Schools and set up his practice as an architect in Bloomsbury Square. In 1862, he moved to a house he designed for himself in Clissold Crescent in Stoke Newington. Commissions for East End churches, including St Chad's, came from fellow parishioners at St Matthias's, Stoke Newington, who established the Haggerston Church Scheme. St Chad's is a good example of Brooks's austere and muscular red-brick Gothic, entirely appropriate for bringing Anglo-Catholicism to Haggerston.

Haggerston

HACKNEY

Hackney Town Hall /330 /A
Old Town Hall /331 /B
St John-at-Hackney /331 /C
St Thomas's Burial Ground /332 /D
London Fields /334 /E
Broadway Market /336 /F
E5 Bakehouse /338 /G
Wilton Way /340 /H
South Hackney /342 /J
Victoria Park /344 /K
The Deli Downstairs /346 /L
Hackney Wick /346 /M
River Lea /348 /N

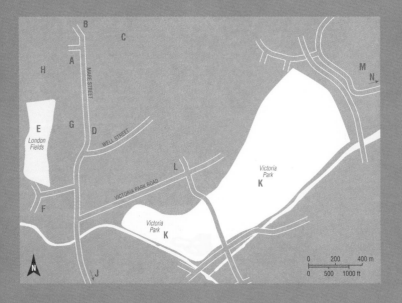

Hackney is a foreign country, stretching a way north of Victoria Park, full of leafy nineteenth-century streets and a popular destination of buses, with big civic buildings round Mare Street, including the Hackney Empire. In the eighteenth century, it was still semi-countryside: a place of large houses, girls' schools, nonconformist chapels and market gardens. Londoners would go out to Hackney to play bowls in the bowling greens at the back of taverns. According to John Thomas, a surgeon who wrote a history of Hackney before emigrating to Cincinnati, 'In 1761 there was one church, three meeting houses, six boarding schools, a free school, a charity school and several almshouses'. But new housing was beginning to creep up the main roads north out of London and, from 1787, a German immigrant, Conrad Loddiges, opened a market garden with hothouses and steam heating. By 1832, there were twenty-three charity schools and five lunatic asylums. In the nineteenth century, with the advent of the railway, the population grew, the streets were laid out with villas, and a silk mill was established in Hackney Wick.

Hackney Town Halls and St John-at-Hackney

My exploration of Hackney begins with the 1930s Town Hall, a grand piece of municipal classicism.

St John-at-Hackney is a fine neo-Greek church by James Spiller.

Christ Apostolic
Church Bethel

The large Victorian church
up the road from the Geffrye
Museum is now a branch of
the Christ Apostolic Church
Bethel, but was originally
opened in the 1860s as
St Columba's, complete
with School, Clergy House
and Mission House next
door. It was designed by
James Brooks. I remember
seeking it out in the early
1970s, inspired by Ian
Nairn's description of it as
'a dusky, grubby working
church that could as well be
in the Ruhr or an industrial
suburb of Paris'.

Then the Old Town Hall,
which I couldn't quite make
out datewise (it's an early
nineteenth-century building
with a later doorway). It's now,
incongruously, a bookmaker's.

St John's has wonderful old
tombstones in the graveyard.

St Thomas's
Burial Ground

In cutting through from
St John of Jerusalem
Church to London Fields,
I have several times been
surprised by the survival of
the burial ground behind the
site of St Thomas's Chapel
on Mare Street, where the
Rev. W. Bates established
a nonconformist chapel
in 1672 on land owned by
St Thomas's Hospital, and
where there is now a Greek
Orthodox church.

Hackney

London Fields

In my recent peregrinations
round Hackney, I have
grown increasingly to
like London Fields, the
curiously shapeless and
essentially nondescript
patch of grass and trees
north of Broadway Market
that people crisscross on
their way to their Saturday
shopping and to the lido
at the north. It's got a
long history as an area
of common ground where
drovers would allow cattle
to graze before taking them
to slaughter in London.
It's surrounded by good
and interesting houses.

Croston Street.

Navarino Road.

And trees.

Hackney

Broadway Market

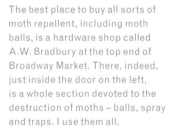

The best place to buy all sorts of moth repellent, including moth balls, is a hardware shop called A.W. Bradbury at the top end of Broadway Market. There, indeed, just inside the door on the left, is a whole section devoted to the destruction of moths – balls, spray and traps. I use them all.

The market is getting smarter and smarter: there's not just a pseudo-old-fashioned butcher called Hill & Szrok...

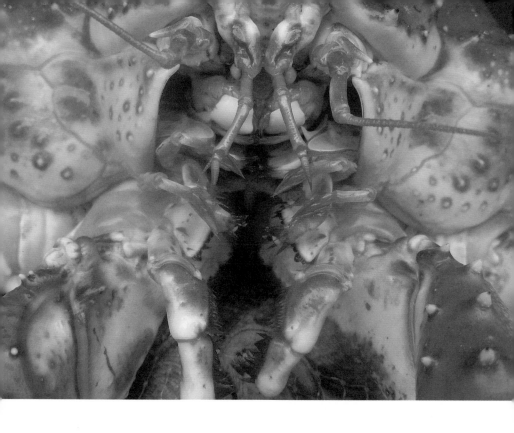

... Now there's also a
fishmonger, Fin & Flounder,
whose giant crab attracts the
attention of passers-by.

E5 Bakehouse

Now that I have penetrated
the mysteries of Hackney,
I can make an early morning
dash to E5, the bakehouse
under the railway arches on
Mentmore Terrace, to stock
up with bread still warm from
the oven.

Hackney

Wilton Way

I read about a Japanese gift
shop in Hackney in *Monocle*.
It's called Momosan and is
on Wilton Way just north of
London Fields. It stocks little
carved wooden tumblers and
spoons from New Zealand
and English ceramics from
the Cotswolds.

Nearly next door is an
equally wonderful shop
called J. Glinert that sells
the best-quality paper
clips and pens, Ghanaian
brushes and books about
the local area.

I was told about the so-called
'discriminatory curve' whereby
consumers become more and
more sophisticated in their
patterns of consumption as
generations pass. These two
shops in Hackney are at the top
of the discriminatory curve.

I went on a wander round
the purlieus of Victoria
Park, beginning with an
investigation of the curious
little graveyard on Globe
Road, which has a single
Soane-like tomb dedicated
'TO THE MEMORY OF
MASTER GEORGE HENRY
SPOONER SON OF
THOMAS WILLIAM AND
FRANCIS SPOONER WHO
DIED THE 25TH JUNE 1822
AGED EIGHT MONTHS'.

It's odd how one can live in
a neighbourhood and miss
areas of it. I don't think I've
walked up Approach Road
since the 1970s and certainly
hadn't seen the ironwork
railings of the London
Chest Hospital.

I was quite taken by this
example of graffiti art under
the motorway flyover.

Victoria Park itself is a tiny
bit too Victorian-municipal
for my taste, but looks fine
when empty in the sun.

I ended up admiring
the skyline of Stratford
across the playing fields
of Mabley Green.

Hackney

Victoria Park

The pagoda in Victoria Park
was originally designed
for a Chinese exhibition in
Hyde Park in 1842, moved to
the newly laid out Victoria
Park in 1847, had a bridge
designed for it by James
Pennethorne, decayed over
the course of the war, was
demolished in the 1950s,
and has only recently been
recreated in the renovations
made possible by the
Heritage Lottery Fund.

I could scarcely bring myself
to record the appearance of
Victoria Park when it was so
ostentatiously, flamboyantly
and nearly nauseatingly
autumnal, like some scene
of the Fall in western
Massachusetts which I've
always thought was to be
avoided. But in the end,
amateur photographer that
I am, I succumbed to
some shots.

Hackney

The Deli Downstairs

A quick excursion in search of Stilton and a Christmas pudding took me to the Deli Downstairs, the headquarters of the Lauriston Road revival, past the long queue for the Ginger Pig and an opportunity to stock up on local ale from the Bottle Apostle.

Hackney Wick

Since I have been told that my blog is too highbrow, I should record the fact that I had lunch in a motorbike store in Hackney Wick following a trip to visit the Custom Built Bicycle Show in the Velodrome. I wanted to like the Velodrome, which is beautiful from the outside, but unexpectedly disappointing inside – cheap finishing, exceptionally poor disabled access and smelling of drains. So, we retreated in search of food in Hackney Wick, where we discovered pancakes, burritos and Beavertown American pale ale (brewed in Hackney) for lunch.

River Lea

Having had a rather
sedentary Christmas,
I decided to get out early
on New Year's Day. I walked
eastwards along the Hertford
Union Canal, not quite sure
which direction to go, and
then headed northwards
up the River Lea beyond
the Olympic Park to where
the landscape resumes
its character of industrial
wastelands.

There were not many people
about; only the woodsmoke
from the canal boats, the
occasional swan, last night's
debris in the pubs, and a
lone sculler. I went as far as
Tottenham Hale. Next time
I must go to Broxbourne.

Further Reading

My introduction to the East End was through
two books that have remained constantly
at my side. The first was Ian Nairn's *Nairn's
London*, first published by Penguin in 1966
and recently reissued, a continual source
of inspiration. The other was Millicent
Rose's *The East End of London*, published by
the Cresset Press in 1951: a deeply poetic
evocation of the history of the East End by
the Marxist daughter of a general in the
Indian army. Equally important has been the
relevant volume of Pevsner's 'Buildings of
England' series by Bridget Cherry, Charles
O'Brien and Nikolaus Pevsner, *London 5: East*
(New Haven and London, 2005), together
with the more specialist preliminary volume
by Elizabeth Williamson, *London Docklands,
An Architectural Guide* (London, 1998). For
the history of the East End, there is now a
wealth of good books. I would especially
recommend Alan Palmer, *The East End:
Four Centuries of London Life* (London, 1989);
John Marriott, *Beyond the Tower: A History of
East London* (London and New Haven, 2011);
and Jane Cox, *Old East Enders: A History
of the Tower Hamlets* (Stroud, 2013). For
architecture, alongside Nairn and Pevsner,
I recommend the relevant sections of Edward
Jones and Christopher Woodward's *A Guide
to the Architecture of London*, first published
in 1983 and regularly updated, and Ken
Allinson and Victoria Thornton's *London's
Contemporary Architecture: An Explorer's
Guide*, first published in 1994 and now in its
sixth edition. I also strongly recommend
The London Encyclopedia, originally
produced by Ben Weinreb and Christopher
Hibbert, and the website *Spitalfields Life*
(www.spitalfieldslife.com), which is a
comprehensive source of information
about all aspects of the East End, including
archival photographs, and now extending
well beyond Spitalfields itself. Otherwise,
my sources of information have been
a motley group of more detailed local
guidebooks, sites stumbled across while
browsing the internet, and the ever-useful
Wikipedia.

Acknowledgments

Several people made me think that the
entries from my blog could be turned into a
book, including Mark Fisher, who has been
a constant source of encouragement, and
Jamie Seaton, the co-founder of Toast, who
realized that the entries could be converted
into a modern equivalent of the Shell Guides.
In putting together this collection of entries
to my blog, I have been helped by many.
Maya Binkin, my Executive and Projects
Assistant, suggested the idea of a blog.
I am deeply indebted to my son Otto, who,
like me, has been influenced by Nairn, but
is much more deeply knowledgeable than
I am about all aspects of twentieth-century
architecture. For many years, I enjoyed
weekend runs with a group from Limehouse:
Monika Machon and Richard Bram, Hazhir
Temourian and Christabel King, and Cynthia
Grant. Beyond these, I am grateful to the
invisible community of people, mostly friends,
who read, and sometimes comment on, the
blog, amongst whom I would particularly
mention Daphne Astor, Leslie Bacon,
Paul Boucher, Linda Brownrigg and
Philip Lewis, Edward Chaney, Rupert
Christiansen, Jeremy Fletcher, Cynthia
Grant, Lavinia Grimshaw, Jim and Ruth
Grover, Dick Humphreys, Joan Keating,
Amanda Kinsman, Toshio Kusamitsu, Candia
McWilliam, Hugh Raven, Keith Thomas and
Marie Willey. It was my literary agent, Maggie
Hanbury, who realized that the book had
commercial potential and encouraged Sophy
Thompson, publishing director of Thames
& Hudson, to take it on. I am grateful to them
both, and to Jen Moore, my editor. Thanks
too to Christopher Foulkes for designing
and editing the beautiful maps, and to Carrie
Segrave for help with editing the text. Most of
all, I want to thank Harry Pearce and his team
at Pentagram for converting inchoate text and
photographs into a beautifully lucid design;
Adrian Shaughnessy who recognized how the
blog could be turned into a book; and Romilly,
who I wish had been able to accompany me
on these, and other, expeditions.

First published in the United Kingdom in 2017
by Thames & Hudson Ltd, 181A High Holborn,
London WC1V 7QX

Map design by Christopher Foulkes

Cartography by Leanne Kelman

Extract on p. 3 taken from *The Companion Guide to
London*, David Piper (rev. edn Fionnuala Jervis,
ISBN 9781900639361) © Boydell & Brewer Ltd

British Library Cataloguing-in-Publication Data
A catalogue record for this book is available
from the British Library

ISBN 978-0-500-51955-4

This book is set in Monotype Grotesque
and Clarendon.

Printed and bound in China by Artron

To find out about all our publications,
please visit **www.thamesandhudson.com**.
There you can subscribe to our e-newsletter,
browse or download our current catalogue,
and buy any titles that are in print.